LIFE WITH UNCLE

Life with Uncle

THE CANADIAN-AMERICAN RELATIONSHIP

John W. Holmes

UNIVERSITY OF TORONTO PRESS

TORONTO BUFFALO LONDON

© University of Toronto Press 1981
Toronto Buffalo London
Printed in Canada

ISBN 0-8020-6460-4

Canadian Cataloguing in Publication Data

Holmes, John W., 1910-
    Life with uncle: the Canadian-American relationship
    ISBN 0-8020-6460-4 (pbk.)
    1. Canada – Foreign relations – United States – History – 20th
century. 2. United States – Foreign relations – Canada – History –
20th century. I. Title.
    FC249.H64   327.71073   C81-095089-8
    F1029.5.U6H64

avec mes hommages de reconnaissance

Jules Léger
1913–1980

Marcel Cadieux
1915–1981

Foreword

Life with Uncle is a revised and updated version of public lectures delivered by the Claude T. Bissell Visiting Professor of Canadian-American Relations in Trinity College, University of Toronto, in 1980-81.

The Bissell professorship was established in 1972 to mark the twenty-fifth anniversary of the Associates of the University of Toronto, an organization of graduates and friends of the university in the United States, with headquarters in New York. It was named in honour of Professor Claude T. Bissell of the Department of English, president of the university from 1958 to 1971 and currently one of Toronto's University Professors. It has brought to Toronto a succession of distinguished scholars, both Canadian and American, and in a number of disciplines. Now lodged in the Centre for International Studies of the School of Graduate Studies, its responsibilities have been extended to include delivering a number of public lectures, which are published here with the assistance of the Associates.

The first appointee under these new arrangements brought high qualifications to the post and was admirably suited to inaugurate the new series of published lectures. After a distinguished career with the Department of

External Affairs, Professor John W. Holmes served for a decade as director-general of the Canadian Institute of International Affairs. He has since taught at the universities of Toronto, York, and Leeds. A shrewd observer of the contemporary scene with a keen sense of history, he is widely respected for his intelligent and balanced perceptions of the intricacies of the Canadian-American relationship. Among his many publications is his recent two-volume work, *The Shaping of Peace: Canada and the Search for World Order 1943-1957*.

ROBERT SPENCER
Director, Centre for International Studies

Contents

'Creation, to me, meant a Creator. And since there was someone so great and powerful that He had created us all, I felt I had better learn His wishes. They were supposed to be good. I wanted to live in harmony with Him – no battle of wills. Yet I also wished greatly to get away and live as I liked.

'If I could have been sure that the Creator was my ally or friend, that would have been a great comfort, in those days. It would have not only saved me from worry, it would have set me free to go about my business with confidence, both in Him and myself. Or if I could have surrendered myself to His rather bleak guidance, that again might have been a relief to me. But – I couldn't do it. I didn't quite trust Him or love Him enough to do that.

'I thought of God as a strangely emotional being. He was powerful; He was forgiving yet obdurate, full of wrath and affection. Both His wrath and affection were fitful, they came and they went, and I couldn't count on either to continue; although they both always did. In short God was such a being as my father himself.

'What was the relation between them, I wondered – these two puzzling deities?'

CLARENCE DAY
author of *Life with Father*,
Life with Mother, and *God and my Father*

Introduction

'There is nothing the matter with Americans except their ideals,' said G.K. Chesterton. 'The real American is all right; it is the ideal American who is all wrong.'[1] Chesterton is too glib, of course. American ideals have inspired millions throughout the world for over two centuries, and they still flash in the dark. There is a sense, however, in which their ideal image of themselves, that they are not as other men, is at war with their common sense and common decency, although it also inspires them to heroic generosity. What they practice is, nevertheless, better on the whole than what they preach. The American contradiction has always seemed to me synthesized in the noble music and alarming words of 'The Battle Hymn of the Republic.' The compulsion to play God is partly self-induced. The Declaration of Independence made clear that this was no ordinary state but a model and a refuge for unhappy people beyond its present writ. It is also, however, a role which has been forced upon Americans by their success and their unparalleled power.

A reason for grave concern now is the relative decline of that power and a soiling of the image, whether it is deserved or undeserved. Rational calculation for a time of transition is distorted by the legend of American omnipotence, the fabrication by friends and enemies of the mythology of world politics manipulated by the CIA, the State Department, and that all-embracing figment, the multinational corporation. The United States is not the only superpower, of course, which regards itself as something more than an ordinary state, but as a model for utopia the USSR has been so conspicuously unsuccessful and its methods of crusading so intimidating that its image is much more tarnished and bloodier than that of the USA. The bipolar world, which has had elements of stability as well as terror, is coming apart at both poles.

As a neighbour it is certainly better to be a Canadian than a Pole, for we have great advantage as well as disadvantage from the giant next door. Still it is an uneasy existence, life alongside an extraordinary power by divine right. The Power isn't really very good at seeing little sparrows fall, and it is difficult just to attract His attention. There are in fact some arguments for not doing so. The ways and means of living our unequal lives has puzzled us for centuries and will continue to do so. We have to do most of the puzzling ourselves because it is a subject that interests Americans only faintly and fitfully. It is with the ways and means past, present, and future that I plan to concern myself in a highly subjective manner.

In the 1980s we are, needless to say, in a critical phase of the relationship between Canada and the United States. We always are. An illusion that goads us is that there is a solution, some understanding that would end all conflict, settle disputes by rule of law or perhaps do away with them altogether. It is somewhat the same illusion as that which bedevils our estimate of the United Nations, the expectation that a mechanism can take over the function of world politics and economics and relieve us of operating it. The first principle to accept is that crisis is normal and more often than not, therefore, no crisis. We should be better equipped, psychically and institutionally, to cope with flaring rows and at the same time to detect long-range factors which threaten the basic equilibrium we have slowly established on this continent over two or three turbulent centuries.

For Canadians there has always seemed to be available, if all else failed, that final solution of continental union, but this cannot, in present circumstances, be taken for granted. The stereotyped assumption that Canada is losing its identity and being inexorably absorbed needs re-examination in the light of a better grasp of history. One might argue that it is because the Canadian roots, political, governmental, economic, and yes, even cultural, are now so deeply entrenched that the final solution has to be ruled out as unacceptable to both parties. The vested interest of Canadians in the maintenance of Canada for the most selfish reasons may now be seen as such that it is the vested interest of Americans to keep us foreign. There are certainly grounds for worry about a loss of cultural self-awareness, but is the problem Americanization or the universal, if regrettable, homogenization of mankind? 'Integration' is no longer regarded as it was in the fifties and sixties as a simple good. Nationalism is now more widely based in both the Canadian and American communities – for better and for worse.

The facts of life in the world at large as well as on this continent threaten a new harshness after several generations of good feeling. As a Canadian official was reported as saying, comparing the time of the Ottawa summit in 1981 with earlier sessions, the world 'has become a meaner and tougher place.' Good feeling is not enough in Canada-US relations. We have needed the hard-headedness to resist the blandishments of hands-across-the-border oratory, but at the same time we have had to recognize the eternal interest of the unequal partner in good feeling and the dangers for us of a descent into ruthlessness. Ruthlessness is, of course, provoked, not just by the competitive stances of our two countries, but by the state of the world: the reduced authority of the United States at large and the accompanying menopausal manifestations; the decline of the West, with us included; and our own need to accommodate an international system which threatens our myopic assumption that North America is an island and that for us the United States is important to the exclusion of all others.

One dilemma is whether to float freer in a world of shifting balances or in self-defence to cast our lot more closely with our overwhelming partner so that we can together be more ruthless to others. The former is clearly the more attractive choice, but choices are limited in a world that gets too damned interdependent.

About a decade ago President Nixon made one of the best speeches an American political leader has ever made about Canada, and he made it in Ottawa. It had the professional touch which American political speeches on this subject so notably lack. It was drafted for him no doubt by the State Department. He made a cogent plea for what he called a more mature relationship. It was a timely response to the feckless kind of nationalism that flourished in Canada at the time. It can be argued, I think, that Canadians have considerably matured since then. We have been sobered by our own reverses. We are less cocky but more confident of our own real strength, less simplistic about the American challenge, less disposed to whine, and more eclectic in assessing the good and bad deeds of the extraordinary power.

It is time to ask, however, whether Americans have similarly progressed in their approach to a country which, the facts of geography and economics suggest, ought to be of primary importance. The political leaders continue to treat us as a child nation, to be humoured with fraternal speeches while our specific complaints are pooh-poohed away. The fact that President Carter visited almost every capital except Ottawa is in itself less enfuriating than the bland American explanation so often offered – that there are not enough problems between us to warrant a visit. There is something refreshing about the concentrated hostility of the *Wall Street Journal*. They do take us seriously, while President Reagan invokes the memory of Mary Pickford to exorcise any differences such fine folks might have.

The powerful and pretentious international relations élite in the United States still pay us no heed. Their serious journals continue to offer at long intervals the token article about Canada, usually written by a Canadian, but rarely if ever a serious, critical study by an informed American of American policy towards Canada. If our stances on Canadian-American relations are immature at times, it is partly because we have so little mature dialogue with Americans. One can only hope that as they realize our increasing consequences for their own prosperity, they will 'absorb us' into their vast educational system. It is a little unnerving, of course, to think of the day when Canada catches on as a hot property in their earnest graduate schools. Our quirks will be fed into a thousand computers. The resultant PhDs, with the total confidence they acquire in those magnificent teaching machines, will seek to rationalize us, unaware that we are not and cannot be a country that makes sense in their terms. Perhaps a little knowledge might be a less dangerous thing. It is hard to say.

The differences we must both take seriously are about the world at large and North America. In the past we have been fairly successful in keeping these concerns apart. As businesslike people we intuitively recognized that although our commerce with each other could by no means be entirely divorced from our foreign policies towards other continents, nevertheless the rules of the game and the considerations involved were *sui generis*. That harmonious assumption has never been severely tested because since the Second World War the Canadian people have never wanted policies abroad which were in flat contradiction with the fundamentals of American policy, although they favoured and pursued quite different ways of going about it. That agreement, however, it should be borne in mind, was not a continental agreement. It was based on a broader alliance and association and, as the record shows, has no more inhibited the foreign policies of Canada than those of Britain or Italy or Australia. That sense of ourselves as part of a community broader than North America has unfortunately diminished in the years of the all-American headlines.

Canadian governments, if not always the Canadian people, have recognized that international institutions, whether they be the UN General Assembly, the NATO Council, GATT, or the Summitry of the Seven, are essential for a country our size to act effectively vis-à-vis a great power. For the bilateral game we have been more sceptical of formalized institutions, groping rather for ways and means appropriate to varying circumstances. These have been, on the whole, sensible guide rules, but guide rules require constant examination, and especially in high tidal times like the present. It is my intention to look at present circumstances, first on the multilateral and then on the bilateral level, to ask what if any changes are needed in our directions, and to grope for a few enduring principles.

My main contention is that although all predicaments are unique, the present must be seen as a phase in a long history. There are remarkable similarities with the situation a century ago when we and the Americans were in angry dispute over the fisheries but firm in the need for transatlantic entente. In those days also we faced US administrations that paid worthy lip service to our right to exist but could not understand why. The historical approach comes more naturally to one who has observed most of this tumultuous century at first hand and knows that things were not better ordered in a golden past. My scope will be limited largely to the postwar world. I shall fix my attention at first on the role of the United States in the new world order as we perceived it when that order

7

was being established and on our fears and hopes for a new era in North America. I shall look at the kinds of institutions that have been and might prove useful to us. Finally I shall suggest that a better understanding of our past should equip us to cope with a relationship which is centuries old and likely to last indefinitely.

History can, as we know, tear countries apart, but in our case I think it can be therapeutic – at least if you accept my version. It must be borne in mind that you are getting the reassessments in tranquillity of a foreign service officer of the postwar era with his particular squint. Mine is, I hope, a valid way of looking at North America, but there is no truth.

1/Also Present at the Creation

Alfonso the Wise, King of Castile, is said to have stated, somewhat immodestly: 'Had I been present at the creation I would have given some useful hints for the better ordering of the universe.' Dean Acheson, who was himself immodest and secretary of state of a country beset by the immodest American dream, found in this quotation the title for his memoirs, *Present at the Creation*. We were all at the end of the Second World War conscious of creating a new and improved world, a system of united nations into which would be fitted in due course bodies such as NATO, the Commonwealth, the Arab League, or the Pan-American Sanitary Organization to perform specific functions within the whole. The American contribution to this creation was unique and critical – the *sine qua non*.

One of the regrettable myths of our time, however, is that the UN was created not by God but by the United States, a distinction which many Americans are still loath to recognize. The myth is compounded by both those who regard US policy as benign and those who consider it malign. There were others present at the creation, notably the Russians, the British, and, to a lesser extent, the Chinese and the French. The product was what they would agree to accept.

9

The lesser powers were also present, none more energetic than Canada, and the institutions which evolved were profoundly different because of the resistance of the small fry to the original pretensions of the great powers. As if in response to Dean Acheson, the Canadian under-secretary of state for external affairs has recently cited John Adams arguing with the British his country's rights in the Atlantic fisheries: 'If heaven, at creation, gave a right it is ours at least as much as yours.'[1] Now the universe is, I think, better ordered because of our useful hints.

If the United States did not dispose, it nevertheless loomed very large as a factor of predominant importance in a new world order. Its presence was certainly welcome, although the implications were baffling. Every country had to find for itself a way of dealing and living with the greatest power on earth. Every country also had to fit that great power into its vision of a global structure which might best guarantee peace and progress – or at least survival. Canada's American problem was not unique but special. Accommodation of a satisfactory bilateral with a multilateral relationship raised for us a wide range of questions.

When the war began in 1939 Canada still rested comfortably, if somewhat neurotically, in the bosom of the Anglo-American entente which had sheltered – and to some extent suckled – us since the trilateral settlement of major disputes by the Treaty of Washington in 1871. Although we too often fancy ourselves as victims of bullying great powers, this triangle was a safety belt and an economic system of considerable value to a country still struggling to subjugate far more territory than its population warranted. We were defended not by the British navy, as was often said, or the US army, which barely existed, but rather by the Pax Anglo-Americana in the seas around us, a régime which most of the world accepted gratefully or resentfully. Our basic commerce was in the triangle, selling more to the British to pay for more goods from the US. It was not a perfect formula, but it could have been worse. Recognition of this triangular system was more in the gut than in the mind. Whereas in 1914 and 1939 we had seemed to be going to war to help out Mother Britain, the very large Canadian war efforts, as distinct from the mere declarations of belligerency, were attributable to our fear that the economic and security system in which we had flourished was threatened. In both cases, the Americans reached the same conclusion after two years effort to resist it. So the Canadian mindset in 1945 was conditioned to prefer a triangle and to see Anglo-America as the most reliable base on which to rest a security or an economic system.

Canada had been in the League of Nations and the United States had not. The absence of the US critically affected the Canadian attitude to the League. It confirmed our fears that it was a Eurocentric institution without the universal power to make collective security a workable policy. US default provided a good excuse and a valid argument for the reluctance between the wars of Canadian governments, Conservative or Liberal, to commit themselves to security pledges. One reason for continuing Canadian, and British, opposition to the collective security provisions of League Article 10 was the hope that without it the United States might join. So the importance of entangling the US in a new League was uppermost in the minds of Canadians when they came to plan the successor body. Canadian perception of the role of the US in world order and in North America was much affected by the course of the war. The belated assumption by the US of leadership in the armed struggle had been greeted by relief and resentment, but mostly relief. As Roosevelt and Churchill, along with Stalin, welded a united nations front, with the great powers specially responsible for the wartime operation, we perceived the shape of a new world organization in which the great powers would continue to lead in peacetime the crusade against aggression. With the US committed, the old arguments for Canadian aloofness from imperial or European entanglements would be answered. It was not the ideal way to run the world, and the prospects of the Soviet Union and the Western powers remaining a harmonious team were less than assured, but it looked like the best chance. Canadian thinking was already strongly functionalist, and it seemed better to build on a team that already existed than to devise a platonic world government and impose it on a turbulent globe. There was an argument also for accepting with its limitations whatever the great powers could agree upon before the war ended and peace fractured their precarious unity.

But the paradoxes in any scheme for international organization were also revealed by the war. To get relatively harmonious great-power leadership in fighting a war was worth concessions by lesser powers, but when the war was over the case would be weaker. Neither

Canadians nor Australians nor other lesser allies had been happy with their allotted place in wartime councils and were determined not to accept it in a peacetime organization. To submit would not only be unjust; it would also permit an unstable kind of hegemony that the rest of the world would not for long accept. It would freeze a system that future great powers would reject. When Roosevelt talked in the early stages of a 'World Council,' consisting, of course, of the great powers at the apex of the new structure, Canada among others resisted. We regarded it as acceptable for the great military powers, on functionalist grounds, to have the decisive say in a Security Council, but not, for example, the United Nations Relief and Rehabilitation Administration to which Canada would be one of the largest contributors. Canada not only wanted to carve out a place for medium powers like itself; it also wanted to break up this hierarchical concept of a world government run by a great-power executive.

We could spot the Rooseveltian messianism in this vision, in spite of our admiration for the man. Roosevelt told King he saw the UN as an expansion of the United States; the United States had become the United Nations, he said.[2] That sounded to a Canadian suspiciously like the dream of 1776 in which the US is not a country like the others but a nucleus round which liberated people – especially the benighted Canadians – would cluster. The world could do with a good dose of American idealism and American muscle, we thought, and the Americans must not be discouraged into retreat. They did have to learn, however, how to live with other countries, especially those of equal moral virtue who made up the Commonwealth,

13

and to accept a UN system that was not neatly run from Washington. When Roosevelt had called the first UN conference at Hot Springs in 1943, he did so on his own and that first multinational Assembly concluded with 'The Star-Spangled Banner' – a somewhat ominous early light at dawn.

The rise of the United States to pre-eminence in the wartime team did teach Canadians certain facts of life about the role of small powers. It was the familiar problem about consultation and commitment that we had hitherto associated with the empire. Romantic historians and politicians have liked to see this as a struggle to wrest control of our foreign policy from the British. Our history was, in fact, an extended exploration of the difficulties of reconciling freedom of action with shared policy-making in an association which we wanted to maintain in our own interests. Regardless of constitutional niceties, Canadian governments themselves made every decision on Canadian foreign policy that they considered important after at least 1867. Nevertheless, a good deal of energy was wasted in the thirties and forties on battling fondly imagined British schemes to drag us into their wars. This phoney war of liberation prevented the public from seeing the problems of large and small powers as inescapable in any context and encouraged on the one hand the 'ready aye ready' formula and on the other the belief that independence was the highest priority in foreign policy, a heresy that was born again a generation later in a different setting.

By the middle of the war, however, this struggle with the 'imperial overlord' to get a voice in the conduct of the war was clarified as the persistent and inevitable problem of relating power to influence, which is and always will be the basic challenge of international organization. We turned to this issue in its new context of three great powers with the benefit of a long and sophisticated experience but trailing some dyspeptic attitudes to great powers in general.

The British, conditioned by their long experience of importunate Canadians, Australians, and South Africans, and the demands of the exiled governments in London, were more amenable to sharing than were the Americans. The Americans realized that colonies would resent dictation from imperial powers, but surely no one would mind the United States, the recognized champion of the peoples of the world, doing what would be best for all. Canadians were particularly angered when the Americans kept saying that they could not admit Canada or Australia to the higher military or supply committees without admitting Brazil. That was, in fact, a real problem for Washington, given its wide commitments, but we were single-minded. Ottawa saw our claim as based on our extended war effort, with which Brazil's did not compare. The new international structures were being plotted along with provisions for the peace settlements before the war ended, and attitudes to the place of lesser powers in peacetime were inevitably conditioned by wartime practices. The Russians were even more adamant than the Americans. Their particular fear was that the Polish government in London would get a seat. In any case, they wanted the UN to be run by the great powers, among whom they would have equal status. What was needed in these distressing circumstances was not just howls of outrage from the lower classes but some serious thought about great-power / small-power relations. In collaboration with other lesser powers we did pursue with some success our functionalist approach to membership of UN bodies and helped to forestall the kind of system which would surely have cracked even before the strident emergence of the Third World.

In wartime, Canada had in fact been somewhat spoiled as a member of what were known informally as the ABC countries. Although we did not have the status we wanted in wartime bodies, our officials had an inside position with Americans and Britons on the economic aspects of the war. In planning postwar financial measures and in preparations for the new functional institutions, in conferences at Bretton Woods, Chicago, or Atlantic City, we were part of an informal directorate of three – a position we retained during the early years of reconstruction and also when NATO was being very confidentially planned. This role as insider was attributable not just to our temporary rank in economic power but largely to the quality of our senior bureaucrats, who were respected in Washington and elsewhere as constructive architects of the new order and not just as Canadian special pleaders. It left us, however, with some illusions.

The war had diverse effects on our alignments. In matters of supply and defence production we were closely associated with the United States, although this was a matter of co-operation and consultative planning under joint direction rather than integration, as it has too often been called. In the summer of 1940 Canada and the

United States had had to look hard at continental defence as a grim necessity. The Ogdensburg agreement of 1940 setting up the Permanent Joint Board on Defence was largely Roosevelt's initiative, but it is wise to remember that this first step on the way to joint continental defence was seen in Canada as a means of getting American support in our war or providing for our own defence in the last resort. There was a flurry of joint planning, which subsided as the military threats moved away from North America by 1943.

Canadian forces, however, had limited contact with the Americans. They had staked out their role on the European front before Pearl Harbor, and there was no good strategic argument for sending them to the Pacific. Consequently, they were not inclined afterwards to challenge the American willingness to assume responsibility for security in that vast part of the globe, especially as participation could not be arranged neatly through an alliance, there being no parallel to the configuration of powers that was to create the North Atlantic alliance. The Arctic frontier was different. The war made Canadians feel vulnerable from the north, and that feeling opened up very complex issues. Effective unilateral defence was inconceivable, but combined defence, which seemed essential, raised delicate issues of sovereignty.

Our trilateral participation in the development of atomic power should not be overlooked. Early in the war we were invited to be partners of the British in an effort that could not be carried on in a besieged island. Co-operation with the United States was ambiguously promised. Inevitably there were acute misunderstandings between London and

Washington, and the few Canadians who knew during the war about this highly secret enterprise had the unhappy experience of dodging fallout. Our refusal to take sides in the bitter postwar controversies between London and Washington reflected C.D. Howe's pragmatic approach to questions of status. He regarded protecting the Canadian interest as more important than getting a seat in high councils. We learned lessons about the risks of lynch-pinmanship which cooled our ardour for a role that had always been more a matter of rhetoric than reality. As a result of our participation, however, Canada was at the end of the war recognized as one of the three 'atomic powers' and took its place as a permanent member of the UN Atomic Energy Commission. Thereby we were launched into high-level diplomacy with a status that could not be maintained but which did earn us respect from the Americans as intelligent, co-operative, somewhat wilful, and not readily subject to dictation.

Whereas Canadians had at first envisaged postwar collaboration in atomic power with the great Cambridge scientists, the British showed little interest in maintaining the joint enterprise. The Americans, in the atomic paranoia which developed, restricted atomic collaboration with any foreigners. So the great Chalk River enterprise, which might well have become another American subsidiary, went its own bold way to produce CANDU. It might be regarded as stellar proof that we can do our own thing superbly if we are forced to rely on ourselves and that we can compete in new technology even with the Americans. It is our bad luck that the particular product is one which has to be judged by values that are not purely economic. Our atomic effort, both in science and in diplomacy, assisted our continuing endeavours to persuade the United States to treat us not blandly and benignly but as a country which, although not in their class, is nevertheless one of the major economic powers of the world. We haven't really made the point yet, but Chalk River helped. It also helped us to mature, for, as Denis Brogan pointed out in 1953, '... the basic Canadian relationship is not either with the United States or with the United Kingdom but with the world of the hydrogen bomb. The very fact that Canada is now one of the treasure houses of the world makes the naive isolationship of the inter-war years ... impossible.'[3]

In the preparation of the peace settlements and the new United Nations, Canada and the other dominions were much aided by the fact that the British, as part of their regular service, kept us well posted on all the great-power negotiations. Equipped with drafts and an intimate acquaintance with what our betters were up to we were in a position to get a hearing in Washington and to make our views known. We felt bitterly that our longer participation in the struggle against Germany had not earned us a voice much louder than what we were accorded. The Americans seemed too little concerned with our demands for justice, but the problem was that they and the British were so acutely involved in exploring any possible ground for consensus with the Russians that they could not upset the chance of agreement by allowing others much of a hand in the planning. We could berate the Americans for insensitivity, but for us also it was of supreme importance that the great powers not fall out.

With American participation, Canada seemed prepared for a new look at collective security, although Canadian politicians and the US Senate were a good deal more cautious about automatic pledges without parliamentary or congressional sanction than the rhetoric of the time and the zeal of some officials implied. Political leaders were bewitched by the idea that collective security was largely verbal and would be assured by an American pledge. It seemed a simple matter of advance promises to oppose aggression without necessarily having troops available – an illusion that persisted until the Korean War faced Canada with the hard decision.

Fear that the US would again back out of the international organization still obsessed the thinking of Canadians and other UN members. It was not until the United States took charge of the UN operation in Korea that this fear was seriously tempered by concern over the consequences of hyperactive US leadership. Familiarity with a US which bestrides the world like a colossus makes it hard for a younger generation to understand the extent to which this concern with American isolationism conditioned our attitudes in the forties. It leaves them prey to the 'revisionist' theorists who grossly exaggerate the American will to empire and accept too readily the accounts by Americans of how they managed and manipulated a new world into existence. American archives have been more easily available than those of other countries, especially the Soviet Union, and American scholars have been more diligent and, of course, better funded. The history of the postwar period has been unwittingly written from a perspective in which the US role is always central.

This is particularly true of those perverse Americans who want to shift blame from the Soviet Union to the United States. Americans, one sometimes thinks, would rather see their own role as diabolical than admit that it was not necessarily decisive. Accepting guilt is also a way of reassuring oneself that history could be controlled. It is certainly true that Americans sought a world order particularly congenial to the United States, but other members wanted US leadership and US resources to be made available and they saw more to be hoped for than feared in the US dream.

Before proceeding, I should explain that my own approach to international institutions is pragmatic and organic, typical perhaps of several generations of Canadian policy-framers. I do not share the romantic view of contemporary cynics and utopians that the UN was immaculately conceived in 1945 and then betrayed. The creation was and is a matter of continuing experimentation, and I believe that what we have now, with all its faults, is infinitely better suited to the real world than what we started out with. The original scheme was tentative and based on some false assumptions. The balance of forces in the world shifted and we have had to adjust, whether or not the shift was entirely congenial. Our failures are attributable to the contradictions in the agenda rather than to faults in the structure or the failure of will on the part of some unearthly abstraction cited too often as 'the United Nations.'

One can identify two deliberate postwar decisions of the Canadian government: to use our status to gain a voice in world affairs rather than to protect us from entanglements; and to seek our security in collective agreements rather than in splendid isolation. Otherwise our policy was a matter of wary adaptation to change we could not control. There was no question, for example, of our having chosen to move from a British to an American camp, as legend has it. The British, as well as we, had to take account of the emergent superpower. We tried in fact to fight the trend and get back to the comfortable old triangular pattern. We were groping for a basis of partnership and co-operation with the United States in widespread endeavours foreign to our previous experience – and that would mean many more clashes of will.

The attitudes of the official community in Ottawa were, of course, not monolithic. There was a healthy debate at all times in the cabinet and within and between government departments. If I generalize somewhat recklessly about what Canadians thought and did, I do so to avoid the boredom of endless qualifications and categorizations. I have my eye primarily on the Department of External Affairs and on those in the East Block whose particular concern was the creation of a new world order.

Sometimes when we had our own clout (much needed relief supplies, financial aid for Britain, uranium and a working reactor, for example) we could have an impact. In the Truman-Attlee-King talks on atomic power in Washington in the autumn of 1945, the Canadians had considerable influence in the development of a Western position on control of the atom. We were concerned not only to press a special Canadian interest. Ottawa was burgeoning with ideas for the brave new world and we wanted a chance to put them forward. It was especially hard to be rejected when we were trying to break with our negativism of the prewar years.

Canadians were only too happy to co-operate with the United States when they were in agreement, as they were on basics, but there was no inclination to form a North American front. We had rejected any suggestion of a united Commonwealth policy, using often as an argument that we did not want to encourage American suspicions of the Commonwealth as a ganging-up. Mackenzie King used our defence ties with the US to quash suggestions for Commonwealth defence strategies, and then shamelessly pleaded in reverse when there was talk of activity in continental defence. We preferred to be one of the middle powers, achieving our ends in alliance with others, but permanently wedded to no one. We were over-confident and had to learn that we could accomplish little in the new institutions without forming coalitions of one kind or another.

In several respects our circumstances put us not 'in the American camp' but in the same predicament as the United States, our interests being not common but coincidental. We were two countries who would come out of the war with increased resources and ready to take off industrially. Much was expected of both of us. We would have to co-ordinate our relief and rehabilitation activities. Canada preferred to do this multilaterally through UNRRA, but the US wanted to run its own show and UNRRA was dissolved. Canada felt more acutely and earlier than the United States the importance of a revived British and European economy for our own economic health. For us the revival of triangular trade seemed vital. Having a more effective system of government than the Americans, we proceeded to provide loans for Britain while American action was frustrated by the paralysis of power over foreign policy in Washington. These loans led us close to bankruptcy in 1947. When Congress did finally approve the Marshall Plan, those friends in the State Department who recognized how we had kept Britain going before they could act managed to arrange a provision by which Marshall Plan funds could be used by the Europeans to pay for their imports from Canada. That action had a critical effect in turning the Canadian economy around and encouraged us to think that quiet diplomacy in the right quarters paid off.

Then came a familiar dilemma. The Americans thought it would be a good idea if Canada participated in the administration of the plan. They tended to think of us first as a country able to share their burden. Here was the old problem faced with the British. There were advantages in having a hand in running the show, but a junior partner could hardly avoid being dragged along by the majority owner and committed thereby. What was more, the rules of the game had already been drawn up by the US. A fixed contribution would be expected. Besides, how would it look to the world if Canada appeared in one of the first major postwar enterprises as a docile member of a North American team? Fortunately there were doubts in Washington also and the idea was dropped. If it had come actually to sharing policy decisions, the Americans would have found it hard to deliver. Their system of government, which leaves the last word to Congress, makes it

24

exceedingly difficult for them to act as an ally, let alone a partner.

It was an element of coincidence in the Canadian and American economic plight that led Canada to support the same strong crusade for freeing the channels of trade and currencies, even though our specific interests often conflicted. Whereas the Europeans and other states, struggling to their feet, needed at least temporary protection, Canadians and Americans tended to be hot gospellers for removing barriers. Canadians had, of course, good reason to be more cautious in inviting free competition to their industrial products or their air routes, and they were therefore more sensitive to the European condition. We saw the need of a transitional period of adjustment but hoped it would be short so that we could trade with Europe and avoid becoming too dependent on the one available market.

It is hard to pin down clear differences between Canadian and American views of what the UN should be. We certainly resisted their preference for a dominant great-power role, but they were tied to what the Russians would accept. US views were not uniform. There were wide gaps between the State Department and Congress, and often we were supporting the internationalists in the State Department against the 'primitives' in the Senate, as Dean Acheson called them. Already we were feeling, as were our allies, the difficulties of dealing with the United States because of the division of powers. Our friends in the State Department could agree with us but they had to tell us that we would have to cater to their Senate if we were to get US support for our causes. It was clear even in the hour of creation that although Americans talked the language of international democracy and equality and thought they meant it, there was a prevalent assumption, especially in Congress, that the US will must not be thwarted by any system. This was not seen in the US as a major problem because of the easy assumption that right-thinking people would recognize US aims as their own.

The very existence of Canada was still hard for Americans to understand, but they were decently respectful of our sovereignty when it was drawn to their attention. It was still widely expected that the Canadians would come round as the bonds of empire dissolved, not as an annexed province but as part of an American cluster. For the Commonwealth the Americans had scant respect and little understanding. They associated it with Commonwealth preferences, which they obsessively regarded as a crime against multilateral economic freedom. During the war they had actually preferred the idea of a unitary Commonwealth so that they could deal only with London, but that didn't work. There was some revival in Congress of the old charge that the British empire had too many votes in the United Nations. When the Commonwealth emerged after the war as a valuable association linking countries of different races and continents in constructive action within a UN framework, the Americans ought to have seen it as a valuable associate in their struggle for world order, but it was hard for them to accept the moral claims of an association to which they did not belong. Canada in particular, and other members as well, were happy, as in the Colombo Plan, to work in harmony with the United States and sought to play down any effort to make the Commonwealth an anti-American front. Nevertheless, this association, which grew more important for Canada after the UN was launched, did serve the Canadian instinct for counterweight. Canadians enjoyed this one forum in which they were free of the large shadow beside them. In the earlier days they saw themselves often as the expositor and perhaps defender of the American position at Commonwealth conclaves, but on many matters the Australians and the British proved more pro-American than they.

Although Canadian thinking about international institutions was on the whole bold, attitudes to a new order in North America was inhibited by several centuries of caution. The prospect of the UN as a factor in Canada-US relations was ambivalent. We did think of the UN as the protector of the weak and, although there was no fear of military aggression from our neighbours, there were economic and cultural aggressions of which even a civilized power or its citizens and corporations could be guilty. We never thought of incorporating our few existing bilateral institutions such as the International Joint Commission into the UN system, even though our prejudice at the time was towards making it all-embracing.

There was some interest in Ottawa in defining our joint defence procedures as regional bodies within the UN. The problem in doing so was the problem that faced NATO when it was formed. If it was to be a regional body in accordance with Article 52 of the UN Charter, its actions were subject to scrutiny by the Security Council and to a Soviet veto. We preferred to describe NATO as a preparation for self-defence under Article 51. The fact that regional bodies could not take security action without the sanction of the Security Council was partly our own doing and reflected some nervousness on our part about US regional hegemony. During the war the US had taken a very arrogant attitude on their right, under the Monroe Doctrine, to exercise surveillance over Greenland and St Pierre when Denmark and France were occupied. We opposed the wish of the Pan American countries to conduct their own security operations on the ground that it was a bad precedent to set. There were other regions of the world with one predominant great power whose zeal to discipline its region had to be checked by the world body.

Regionalism was a feature of a new world order much discussed, and it appealed in many ways to our preference for functional bodies that could act together. On the whole, however, we opposed regionalism, partly because of a certain devotion to the one-world dogma of the time and our strong conviction about the need to maintain transatlantic unity, and partly because we were not very comfortable in any region into which we would be shoved. The Western Hemisphere was less real to us than the Northern, and we felt little in common with the Latin Americans. Membership in the OAS we rejected for various reasons but largely to keep out of American quarrels with their Latin associates. We fought a particularly long battle against being incorporated into the Western Hemisphere regional grouping of the World Health Organization.

As for North America on its own, that was no region but a disparate dyad, a euphemistic term political scientists later found for a very disproportionate coupling. UN bodies could be helpful, however, to protect us against the thrust, the sheer vitality of the United States economy, particularly in its postwar mood of assuming that what was good for General Motors was good for the world. The General Agreement on Tariffs and Trade was essential in getting US tariffs scaled down. A notable case also was the international régime of the air reached in Chicago in 1944. It was based on a principle, the so-called Four Freedoms, of which Canadians were the special advocates. Without such a régime Americans, with their vast available air power, could have cornered the major air routes of the world including those in Canada.

To cope with the United States we often needed company, and we early learned the arts of building voting blocs of the like-minded for this purpose. There were grounds for caution, nevertheless, in looking to international institutions to regulate the US. Many members of the UN were in those days more dependent than we on American largesse and they would think twice about taking sides against them. We were, of course, vulnerable ourselves in international bodies, for we clung to protective devices which were at least as restrictive as those of the US and as likely to be in conflict with the international rules of the game.

In the emergence of the Cold War and the establishment of NATO the role of the United States has also been much exaggerated by friends and enemies alike. The growing fear of the Soviet Union after the war, based on both valid and invalid perceptions, was a phenomenon in all Western Europe and North America, as well as other continents. The Canadian conclusion, that collective security within the UN would not work and that it must be supplemented by provisions for collective defence in a Western alliance, was reached by deduction from evidence and opinion of all kinds and from all available sources. It was not, as too often said, an American view thrust upon us. For one thing, there were as many positions on the subject in the United States as elsewhere.

Fear for the stability of Western Europe after the Prague coup of 1948 drove all Western leaders to consider what should be done. Various schemes for West European alliances or American guarantees were under consideration. An approach from the British got Canada into the action. Together they met with the Americans for confidential discussions and the drafting of terms for an alliance to be discussed later with the Europeans. The Canadians favoured the formation of a community rather than the simple American guarantee of the European countries which many Americans and Europeans would have preferred. Canada, for one thing, wanted a multilateral association in which could be encased the continental defence provisions which were being somewhat hesitantly worked out with the Americans. The encasing may have been more symbolic than consequential, but it made Canadians feel more comfortable. Our membership of NATO did serve the vital purpose of transforming what might have been a simple American aid-to-Europe scheme into a defence community, which was much more likely to endure on an equitable basis.

Canada's well-known anxiety to include Article 2[4] was intended not to convert NATO into an economic institution but to extend the concept of alliance to the harmonization of economic policies. The Americans had no real objection to this assumption, but they feared that the article would be misinterpreted by the Senate. The latter was worried about any kind of indefinite commitment to economic support of Europe. Canadians were exceedingly worried lest the very different economic predicaments of Europe and North America after the war lead to alienation. Contrary to traditional interpretations, I believe that Article 2 has been observed about as much as one could have expected. There have over the years been continuing efforts to restrain, in the interest of allied unity, the fiercer prosecution of transatlantic economic conflicts. Nothing proved US commitment to Article 2 more dramatically than the Marshall Plan. No article could abolish the divergent interests of NATO members. It could simply plead for restraint and awareness. The record could have been a great deal worse. It is the spirit of Article 2 which motivates the summit meetings of the seventies and eighties.

There were Canadian hawks and American doves, but on the whole the Canadian attitude to Soviet policy and Soviet intentions was less categorical. There were more doubts. We tried immoderately to be moderate. Canada advocated NATO as a precaution against what Soviet policy might prove to be; and Canadian diplomats, especially Dana Wilgress, the ambassador in Moscow, were perhaps more sensitive than either the State Department or the Foreign Office to Russian fears, however unfounded. We were less convinced that the Communist International was a monolith, although it seemed prudent to assume that it might act in unison. I recall, for example, that when we at the Canadian embassy in Moscow detected in the press evidence in the spring of 1948 of trouble between Moscow and Belgrade, we could not convince the American or British experts who were set in the view that nothing favourable is possible, an attitude to which NATO specialists still cling. Later, while again recognizing the probability that China and the Soviet Union were together behind the North Korean invasion in 1950, Canada opposed US polemics which, in its view, would consolidate this unity.

We were less inclined to attribute all revolutionary activity, especially in Asia, to Moscow's direction and to regard that continent as a very complex area of the world. Communism as an ideology was certainly not regarded with a friendly eye in Ottawa, but the objections were more liberal than capitalist. It was the threatening behaviour of communist states and their denial of the human rights even of their own citizens rather than their discredited economics which drove Canada into hostility.

Canadians might in retrospect be called premature détentistes. We did not see the overthrow of the communist régimes, however desirable, as a practical proposition and argued in fact for co-existence, although the word had to be shunned as long as it had been appropriated as a slogan by Moscow. Our view of China was much more aloof than that of Washington. In spite of American arguments, the Canadian cabinet decided in June 1950 to negotiate with the People's Republic of China for diplomatic relations. Unfortunately the Korean War broke out two days later and circumstances postponed the carrying out of that policy for twenty years. Americans, whose eyes have seen the glory, feel a stronger urge to trample on sin, possibly because they have a greater capacity for trampling. Canadians suffer more often from the delusion that human wrongs in other countries can be righted by a strong speech or a stiff note from the Canadian ambassador.

When a military stalemate had been reached in Korea at about the status quo ante bellum, Ottawa argued for armistice and the patient effort to reunify Korea by peaceful means. We pointed out that the UN side was not in a position to demand unconditional surrender even though it was morally justified in doing so. One simply had to accept the continuing existence of régimes one did not like. Above all we feared that the impetuosity and moral fervour of some Americans would get them into a hopeless land war in Asia, a fear that led us to support the armistice of 1954 in Indochina and accept a thankless position in the control commissions in spite of American scepticism.

Canada shared with the United States and its other allies certain basic attitudes to Soviet policy which brought them together in NATO. They were, however, less inclined to see the rest of the world in Cold War terms. The difference was in perspectives and largely about tactics. It can in part be attributable to national temperament, although that is uncertain ground for objective assessment. I sometimes think Canadian political leaders opted for the less pessimistic interpretations of Soviet policy at least partly because they were thereby relieved of problems involved in defence expenditures and the raising of forces. Perhaps also it was easier for us to argue for patient negotiation with the Russians because, unlike the Americans and the British, we had little experience at first hand of the exasperation and frustration of doing so. It was more appropriate also for a lesser power, without decisive responsibilities, to retain its uncertainties than for the great powers on whose capacity to respond if necessary we were all dependent.

It was healthy, however, to have small, middle, and great power assessments, as well as a second view from North America, fed into the NATO calculations. Some Americans, and even more Europeans, were supercilious about the heresies of Canadians and other lesser peoples in the North Atlantic community, but there was no undue effort to shut us up. There were always those in Washington, London, or even Paris who agreed with us – particularly over the necessity of avoiding war with China or the folly of promising the 'liberation' of Eastern Europe. Our influence, such as it was, was effective as co-operative allied pressure in sustaining those in Washington we agreed with. It is a mistake to describe the exercise of influence among states as if they were billiard balls.

The United States was not in our eyes or those of the other allies an equal partner. It had the decisive clout. When it came, for example, to the decision whether or not to respond militarily to the North Korean attack, we could not tell the Americans what to do with their own troops. We could advise them not to intervene but not the reverse. We could agree to help out, and this Canada was in no position to do for we had no troops to spare in June 1950. We felt obliged to support the UN operation in

Korea because of our fear that the UN would go the way of the League if it failed to act. That operation had to be under US command because there was no other way of avoiding swift defeat for the UN cause. We were the last of the major allies of the US to produce an armed force, and it arrived almost too late for the fighting. Although in taking its delayed and reluctant decision to send forces the government was certainly aware of Americans' criticism of their allies, the decision was fundamentally one to support the United Nations, not the United States. As acting Canadian representative at the UN at the time I was instructed to discourage American-inspired requests for a Canadian contribution as these would be counter-productive.

Respecting US leadership did not mean agreeing with all aspects of US policy. We insisted on UN control of the war policy in hope that there could be independent judgments – over the crossing of the 38th parallel or going provocatively close to the Chinese border, for example. Something, however, was owed to the leader. Some allies were more docile than we in accepting this principle, but we all in the end believed that the strength of the alliance was our own defence and as we were engaged in an exercise in deterrence those whom we feared should not be misled by our internal differences.

When, after the Chinese entered the Korean War, the Americans were hell bent for denouncing them for aggression, Mr Pearson argued vigorously and loudly against such a step as unhelpful because it was important at that point to negotiate an armistice with the Chinese. We were clearly not going to defeat them, and calling them aggressors, whether justified or not, was no way to get them to stop fighting. In his view, furthermore, the Chinese intervention might well have been a defensive reaction, as the Indians had warned us. We lost that argument not only to the Americans but to the other powers involved in the UN force and then voted with the majority for the resolution. In doing so, however, Mr Pearson said that we had not changed our minds on policy. We wanted to make clear that the allies would stand together when the chips were down. Perhaps we should have stood our ground, but the decision not to do so was a matter of principle defined in explicitly functional terms. Mr Pearson eschewed rude diplomacy, but he alternated quiet with loud diplomacy to serve his purpose.

When the UN, in the late forties and fifties, settled into an active pursuit of peaceful settlement and economic development, Canada was at the height of its middle power. Although that role has been exaggerated and simplified, it cannot be dismissed. It was based on a reputation for resourcefulness and objectivity, without pretence of non-alignment. Our association in alliance with the United States may at times have weakened our efforts to play the honest broker, but it also gave Canada status as a lesser power assumed to be not without influence.

To understand our diplomacy it is essential to shed the persistent myth that the United Nations was a tool of the United States and that the Americans could always get their own way. The scene was not polarized between super-powers. Positions and actions now ascribed simply to the US were usually those of the West in general. We thought of ourselves as part of a Western team rather than as an associate of the United States. There was no doubt that the US was far and away the most powerful member. There were not many important causes that could be carried without American support, but the US could by no means always get its own way. Arms were twisted, but not even the Latin Americans could be counted on for unquestioning support without substantial concessions to their wishes.

We were subjected often to strong but legitimate argument. I cannot recall during the fifteen-odd years I was involved at the UN explicit threats seriously intended, although a lesser power inevitably feels some implicit threat when opposing a powerful neighbour. When the US did get a resolution through Council or Assembly it was nearly always a resolution that had been considerably altered to get the support of others. The most notable defiance of the United States was led by Canada in 1955 when Paul Martin took over the leadership of a lesser-power revolt to promote the package deal that brought into the UN all the outstanding applicants hitherto blocked by East and West. We persisted in spite of the fury of John Foster Dulles and the empty threats of Henry Cabot Lodge. Our action was about as consequential as anything ever done to shape the UN. There were those who thought and still do that the UN was wrecked when the doors were opened to almost any applicant. Certainly the Assembly became a less congenial place, but the United Nations flourished because it came to reflect the real world and encompass its problems. Does anyone think we would be better off today if the Third World were conducting its campaigns outside the United Nations?

A judgment as to what the United States thought of Canadian attitudes depends, of course, on what Americans one is talking about. I think it fair to say that our activities gained us respect from what one might call the liberal internationalists. There were those on the right who regarded Mr Pearson as being under the baleful influence of Delhi or even Moscow. That was not the case of John Foster Dulles who, although he did not like many of the things Mr Pearson did or said, recognized that he had been a founder and remained a staunch supporter of NATO. After ten years some Americans were beginning to understand a little better the behaviour of these strange Canadians. Early illusions that, when they had broken loose from Westminster, they would prove not only right-minded but like-minded had been shattered in the forties. General McNaughton in the UN Atomic Energy Commission had refused to knuckle under to Bernard Baruch. Then when the US had pressed an unwilling Mackenzie King to let Canada take a place in 1948 on the UN commission to arrange elections in Korea, assuming that the Canadians would be good guys, they found that neither the Canadians nor the Australians were going to agree with US policies automatically. Over Palestine and other issues, however, they were also finding out that Canadians balancing in the middle could be useful in promoting accommodations. Contemporary diplomacy had need of Canada the middle power, and the Americans helped invent that phenomenon.

For Canadian diplomats one of the attractions of UN diplomacy was its sheer multilateralism. We could work in coalitions to deal with the United States from greater strength, being true to our convictions and loyalties discriminately. One could agree or disagree with them and often assist in their difficulties with antagonists. The relationship with the United States was much healthier and less suffocating than critics have assumed. In our basic alignment we stood with them not by compulsion but of our own free will. Our identity was clear to us and to others and we were not beset by the obsessions on that subject which have stultified the free thinking of a later generation. The policy of a small power is no less independent because it decides to be an ally rather than an abstainer.

2/Shaping the Continent

Having looked at the ambiguity in Canadian attitudes to the United States role in the world after the Second War, our wish for American leadership and anxiety about the direction it would take, I would now like to concentrate on the bilateral relationship on this continent during that period. There is more continuity over the centuries than we are inclined to think, but there are at present serious questions to be asked about trends and mutations. In seeking appropriate shapes for the continent we find the same ambiguities, the advantages and disadvantages of living with this particular superpower and the contradictions involved in any efforts to regularize or even describe our unconjugal state. The trouble with talking about the United States in confident generalities is that it is a kind of Jekyll and Hyde phenomenon, except that it is rarely as Jekyllian as Americans like to think and very rarely as Hydean as its critics allege. Basically, thank God, it is human.

Whenever there are troubles, it is said, we look to institutions for a solution. Not surprisingly, therefore, the North American air is alive with rumours of new patterns for the continent – common markets, free trade areas, a trilateral Canada-US-Mexico accord, as suggested by

President Reagan, or even a 'Treaty of North America' under consideration by the National Governors Association of the US, unions and combinations joint or conjoint, alliances entangling or enfranchising. Most of them are guaranteed by their advocates to leave both countries utterly sovereign and utterly identifiable, although some assume that homogenization is a good thing. Sovereignty is something Canadians worry about, but they agonize about their identity. Americans worry against all reason about their sovereignty, to the utterness of which every senator is dedicated. The threat to their identity could be that, having Americanized the world, they can no longer call their soul their own.

There is a certain backs-to-the-wall desperation in the sponsorship by the new US administration and assorted politicians of a pan-continental accord. There is some sense of desperation also in the tone of those Canadians who are seeking in continental schemes new ways and means of reviving economies which look a good deal less buoyant than they did when North Americans (those above the Rio Grande) were top dog. Canadians continue to assume that Americans, having never really abandoned their manifest destiny, would accept without much demur any proposition of ours for what is called indiscriminately 'economic integration.' It is advisable, however, to bear in mind the comment of one of the best American experts on Canada, Sperry Lea, who asked in reference to current proposals for formal free trade arrangements 'whether the policy option which for Canadians "will never die" is one that will ever really live for Americans.' It is wise also to use the word integration with great care, as it has become both loaded and hopelessly imprecise in common usage.

Canadian-American relations did not begin yesterday, and it is necessary first to look briefly at their slow evolution. Because a good deal of the confusion in recent controversy is based, in my opinion, on a misreading of postwar trends and policies, I should like to offer first a few conclusions of my own about a time that I experienced and which I have recently re-examined. A certain mythology has grown about government policies in that period which, although it is now less dogmatically embraced by serious scholars, has become embedded in textbooks and other manifestations of the folk tradition. The gist of my case is that continentalism, as it has been called, was more like a force of nature. The effort of governments, in agreements reached with the United States, was to control and discipline that force rather than to encourage it. My conclusion from this interpretation is that rules, commitments, or even institutions established between Canada and the United States, while designed to reduce conflict, are not necessarily intended to bring us closer together, as the saying goes. Their purpose, rather, is to regulate forces which, unless a Canadian place is staked out, would inevitably erode our sovereignty and our identity.

Precedents go back much further than the Second World War. Jay's Treaty of 1794 introduced the concept of joint commission and arbitration, a note of fairness and rationality that persisted through a century or more of often violent controversy. Our folkloric belief on dubious grounds that the British let us down in all the boundary disputes obscures the fact that the Americans let us, with vastly inferior power and population, grab over half the continent. After the Americans' Civil War we amalgamated scattered settlements from coast to coast to strengthen ourselves against the threat from the South. In fact we made ourselves thereby more vulnerable, but we had to trust the American respect for constitutional authority. Our defences were plate glass.

The Americans were understandably loath to accept the existence of the Dominion of Canada which President Grant referred to as 'this semi-independent and irresponsible agency.' It was not until the beginning of this century that sage men on both sides, and in Britain as well, decided to draw up the Boundary Waters Treaty of 1909, a set of agreed principles and joint mechanisms for dealing with one group of contentious issues along the common frontier. It was a triumph of those quiet but influential elements in the United States who believe in the higher principles of the republic over the Hydean swaggerers. Without those Jekylls – or that benign element in Americans at large – Canada would not have survived.

Conflict and competition are natural and inevitable between two countries situated as we are. Our virtue rests in the means we contrive to cope with them. The weaker power is just as likely as the strong power to be unfair in its claims. Nevertheless, it has a special need to appeal to the stronger power's ultimate sense of fairness and rough justice, because it can be crushed, even inadvertently. Most Canadians would agree that Americans as individuals have been as fair and just as any people on earth. The increasing problem has been the extent to

44

which a great country, burdened with a non-responsible system of government, can manage to follow its better instincts.

We can take some comfort from historical recollections of the times in the past couple of centuries when, after an accumulation of festering grievances, an awareness reached the highest levels of the consequences of breakdown. There would follow the appointment of a joint commission, a conference, or an exchange with the president, a round of settlements and a fresh start. A channel to the upper levels in Washington always seemed important for Canada in coping with the American system. The Americans have a galling habit of regarding us as a regional aspect of a national problem. Even our standard joint institutions, the International Joint Commission and the Permanent Joint Board on Defence, worked better when the American chairman could get on the phone to FDR or Harry or Ike. We are told that the Jimmy-Pierre phone was in frequent use, but the White House by then had lost or mislaid its power to dispose.

Settlements have been largely specific in our pragmatic tradition. For practical people ad hoc institutions, special commissions or conferences, third-party arbitration in particular cases, seemed better suited or more easily agreed upon than standing bodies. A very few permanent institutions were set up. The most notable was the International Joint Commission, linked to the Boundary Waters Treaty. It has been successful to date because its scope is specific, its reach not exceeding its grasp. It was a brilliant formula to cope with certain dealings between two unequal states. Being joint means that it is really two commissions, one in Washington and one in Ottawa, with two chairmen. Three members from each country, acting together, seek to find agreed solutions to border problems which they recommend to the two governments whose sovereign right to decide is not questioned. That formula, which has been copied in other bodies, temporary or continuing, is more important than the IJC itself.

Becoming allies during and after the Second World War added an element of solidarity to a relationship which for centuries was barely cordial. It provided a commitment to each other's sustained health, but it has also provoked bitterness from false expectations. Our defence production sharing arrangements lapsed quickly at the end of the war when there was no common cause and our natural state was revealed as competitive. They were revived, however, when we joined forces in NATO. Being allied puts a brake on cut-throat competition but that is all. It is a mistake to think of our participation with the Americans in an alliance as giving us special economic advantages, but it is wise to contemplate the disadvantages we would suffer if we were outside the alliance.

At the end of the Second World War Canada and the United States became, in their respective classes, leaders in the creation of new institutions for world order. There was little interest on either side, however, in creating new institutions for the continent. The IJC would, of course, continue. So would the PJBD. It had been set up in 1940 on the pattern of the IJC as an advisory body to avoid conflict and to mull over, for the respective governments, mutually agreeable military plans. Although the co-ordinating mechanisms for war production were dismantled in

46

1945, the bureaucrats and the military had set up informal and effective patterns of co-operation, often by telephone, which have ever since provided a broad infrastructure for management of complex interrelations.

The importance of this unstructured transgovernmental system is acknowledged, its value and its risks constantly assessed, but it has worked better without being defined and prescribed. If it has provided a form of institutionalization not to be found in the charts, it is very much in the pragmatic and functionalist tradition. These undefined contacts enabled Canada to avoid injuries – often inadvertent – and secure arrangements that could never have been negotiated on a higher level. At the same time they may have eroded national direction of the economy, particularly as there has grown up a vast web of state and province expedients which are hard to control. One of the causes of our present discontents, however, is that the freedom of the nice American bureaucrats to be helpful is increasingly limited by the restrictive and protective measures of Congress. On our side greater attention by Ottawa to national strategies – communications, cultural, or industrial – and the increasing number of our international commitments have required closer surveillance also of our free-wheeling officials.

The fact that this kind of co-operation was possible did relieve the pressure for more formal bodies. Canadians were not eager to create more precise institutions. There was the traditional fear of mortgaging our political sovereignty. We were particularly uneasy after the war when we were faced with the unforeseeable consequences of greater reliance on North America for economic and security reasons because of the paralysis of Britain, Europe, and our other traditional counterforces. This nervousness was dramatically displayed by Mackenzie King in 1948, when our desperate balance of payments turned our attention to desperate solutions. After having authorized secret talks by officials about a possible free trade arrangement with the US, King abruptly cancelled them because he concluded, with some advice from beyond this sphere of our sorrows, that we would thereby lose our souls and be gobbled up by the Americans, who, he said, had never forsaken their aspiration for a united continent. This ambivalence about continental institutions persists – and rightly so.

Our attention at the time was on universal rather than continental institutions for collective security and monetary and commercial discipline. The United States was even more concerned with world-wide systems and not inclined to think of Canada very much at all. Canadian and American views on the kind of world order we wanted were largely coincidental, although our national interests were by no means always comparable or even compatible. Canada saw great advantage in universal systems – GATT, for example, which would discipline the United States. We did not expect to appeal to the UN to restrain American military aggression, but we might well want to appeal to various international agencies against American economic policies – being somewhat more dimly aware that we could also be appealed against ourselves.

There was little disposition, however, to invite UN inspection of or intervention in our common-law life in North America. When we became engaged in continental defence plans there was anxiety, as mentioned earlier, to register them as UN regional arrangements, and later as part of the NATO framework. However, we went along, not too reluctantly, with the American insistence on keeping North American defence separate from and free from interference by European allies. Other countries showed little interest in the management of internal North American relations, and we came to see that our inter-connections were of such intensity that, even within a world-wide system, we would still have to find special ways and means of working with our giant neighbour.

The evolution of the defence relationship illustrates the real value for Canada of institutions of the right kind. This point has been obscured by the tendency to regard the United States as the prime initiator of continental defence. The US military in fact regarded the North as a diversion. The Canadian front was, in any case, usually seen in Washington as a minor element in more important matters, including their own inter-service rivalries. Whether or not our fears of the Soviet Union were justified, Canada saw itself in a new air age as open at the top. Conscious of having much larger territorial responsibilities than we could afford to cope with on our own, we wanted help from our powerful neighbour. We saw the looming confrontation as one between us – that is, the West or the 'free world' – and the Russians rather than as a bipolar struggle between the two giants. There was less disposition, therefore, to worry about our being drawn into an American conflict, even though we worried about American brashness.

We had our prewar pledge to live up to. In return for Roosevelt's promise in 1938 not to stand idly by if Canada were attacked, Mackenzie King had said we would not allow an enemy to attack the US by way of Canada. That was more easily said than done. The Americans, for their part, had vivid memories of 1940 when Canada, having involved itself in a war without the means to defend itself, had, after the fall of France and what seemed an imminent fall of Britain, turned to the US for help. We felt, of course, and with justification, that we were fighting America's war, but, in Washington's eyes, we had done so without having adequate defences of our own. We put them in a difficult spot when in 1940 we had to send all our naval vessels off to defend our last outpost, Britain. They had not enough to defend themselves, let alone us.

After 1945 Canada opted for collective defence in its own interests and because there was no alternative. We could not leave our vast territories unattended without risking our sovereignty over them. There was also the persistent fear that if we did not contribute adequately to our own defences, we would be faced with irresistible pressure from the Americans to do it for us. We could have bravely tried to manage for ourselves, but the cost would have been astronomical.

In calculating what we should expect of our allies, it is well to bear in mind that no one ever forced us to take over responsibility for far more land than we could ever control. Doing so had been the consequence of a very uncharacteristic recklessness and imperial instinct on the part of our own forefathers. Goldwin Smith thought it was a fatal mistake to stretch our mandate beyond the Lakes, and I sometimes wonder if he was right.

This collective and specifically continental defence was not so much the deliberate choice of a Canadian government as an irresistible conclusion. The problem for the government was to control defence in such a way that Canada and Canadian forces would continue to exist as such. We had paid the Americans for their bases in Canada at the end of the war to make sure they departed, and we were not disposed to invite them back. There must be rules and understandings to protect a distinct place for Canadian forces and put restraints on American action, while making sure that Canada, as well as the US, was adequately defended. We had in place the Permanent Joint Board on Defence based on the joint principle and with a purely advisory role. We proceeded to institutionalize the principles and practices of defence co-operation much more categorically than in any other areas of common interest, probably because of its sensitivity for a sovereign state.

In 1947 there was a joint statement of the two governments on the rules guiding defence co-operation. A Joint Industrial Mobilization Committee was set up by an exchange of notes in 1949. To make sure, as in the Hyde Park agreement of 1941, that the Americans would not do all the supplying and the Canadians all the buying of arms, there have been various renewals of the defence production sharing principle. These did lead to some rationalization of production, but there were never grand plans for a continental defence economy. They simply gave Canada access to the American market in arrangements which a student of the subject has called 'a sort of barter.' There were various other joint bodies, ad hoc provisions for radar chains, and the like, and in 1950 the definition by exchange of notes of Principles for Economic Co-operation,[2] having the common defence effort in mind.

Eventually the logic of effective joint defence led to NORAD in 1957. The North American Air Defence Agreement is not, as often assumed, a Canada-US military alliance, but rather a consequence of the alliance. It is merely a provision in advance for the co-ordination of the two forces at the operational level in the event of an attack on the continent. The pressure for NORAD came more from the Canadian than the American military, and the latter have seemed in later years less committed than we are to its continuance. Canadian territory is less important to the US in the missile age and there are those in the Pentagon who see advantage in managing continental air defence without having to worry about the sensitivities of foreigners.

Certainly the implications of NORAD were more integrative than what had gone before but no more so than the military provisions of NATO for its members in general. It can be argued, however, that NORAD provided a framework within which there was staked out the role and rights of Canadians, an intention strengthened by subsequent alteration of the structure to create a separate Canadian region. The alternative, after all, is an unplanned situation in which the Americans, if the balloon went up, might expect to be able to move in as they willed. Even if Canada were to declare itself neutral and withdraw from NATO, it is doubtful if we could disengage ourselves from the defence problems of a country from which we cannot be towed away.

Those who oppose a military association with the United States make an error in calling for the abolition of NORAD, which is merely a mechanism to guarantee our position in a state of alliance. They should go back to Ogdensburg, NATO, and the agreements of the forties on which the alliance is based. There are many reasons for asking whether the specific NORAD agreement is applicable to the present strategic predicament, but there remains, under any circumstances, a strong argument for drawing up with the Americans some rules and understandings by which they as well as we must abide. It seems to me a mistake, therefore, to regard this series of defence agreements with the United States as in themselves representing the will of a government towards continental integration. They are, in fact, an essential form of resistance to a fate with might not be worse than death but certainly a kind of euthanasia.

Defence was, of course, special because although the perspectives, roles, and interests of the two countries were distinct, there was the common cause. There was a common cause in the world economy but also fair competition to be provided for. That cause has of late been strengthened, however, by the need of allies to share diminishing resources among themselves and to meet the challenge of the Third World on some common ground.

For the kind of unstructured but mannered régime which held sway by the fifties one might use the term 'constructive and harmonious co-operation,' words used by both parties in the exchange of notes in 1954 on the St

Lawrence Seaway. It was an ideal, of course, rather than a precise definition, a sweet formula which could be useful for the junior party, provided it kept the wool from its eyes. In maintaining the régime the IJC has often been helpful in examining grievances and proposing compromise, but it was never intended to replace negotiation between governments. The joint bodies can sort out the basic elements, but political leaders have to cope with the struggle for advantage. The Seaway, it should be noted in passing, is not a single authority but conforms to the joint pattern. We have, in fact, two seaways which harmonize their activities.

Of governmental negotiation there has been a great deal: pushing and pulling, hollering and counter-hollering, quiet diplomacy when that was more effective, infinitely protracted bargaining, wheeling and dealing. This must be regarded as all quite normal between civilized states, provided there is a reasonable balance in the outcome. Scholars who have actually tried to keep score seem to think it has been reasonably equitable so far. Canada has certainly done more than survive.[3] In the case of the Seaway, Canada forced the US hand by deciding to go it alone when the US Congress, dominated as usual by regional interests, continued to be obstructive. On the Chicago Diversion of water from the Great Lakes to float its garbage we got our way with the help of the State Department and vetoes by the president. On the Columbia River we did less well as we were hampered by the lack of a clear strategy and internal division between Ottawa and Victoria. On the Chicago and St Lawrence issues it was the Americans who were divided. Our interests coincided with those of many American states and we had support in Washington. The Americans were united over the Columbia. (It is worth recalling that they did at least come around to our view, nevertheless, drawn from concepts of international law about the need for equitable apportionment of downstream benefits.) There were hundreds of other issues, from ground fish fillets to trucking in bond across Ontario, hassles over immigration and customs routines, without any fixed pattern and few mechanisms except that bureaucratic network and the diplomatic process at all levels.

On both sides we avoided linking issues. The American government machine was too incoherent to formulate a co-ordinated Canadian policy in which fish or pork would be bargained for gas or relations with Cuba. Canadians have so far sensed that linkage was a game that would inevitably be won by the stronger power. Linkage cannot, however, be avoided on a human basis. Canada, the good ally, got more generous treatment in Congress than a Canada regarded as too friendly with Castro and Mao. A highly political animal like L.B. Johnson was ready to offer help on the auto pact when Canada had been helpful over Cyprus. To link is human, and senators inevitably get border television, for example, mixed up with convention expenses. Canadian policy has not been submissive, but our actions are tempered by a steady realization that things go better when the mood across the border is amiable.

From time to time commissions for investigation or recommendation were set up, almost always on the joint principle. The rational relationship has been hampered somewhat by a stubborn American conviction that nice

55

people don't have conflicts and it is mischievous to draw attention to them. Such naïve expectations lead only to inept solutions and recriminations. Joint investigatory bodies can be helpful, as for instance when, after the row over the sudden American imposition of a surcharge on imports in 1971, and ad hoc commission reached agreement on a common set of statistics. In most of the arguments, however, it was not simply a question of judicial investigation of rights or even simple equity based on the status quo. We were each legitimately struggling for gain, and in Canada's case we were constantly striving to alter the present ratio of GNP on the continent. That is why we have been shy of suggestions for a continental energy policy, which seemed to imply – though they need not – a division of present resources on the basis of present population or GNP. Laurier, we thought, was premature. The twenty-first century is to be ours.

Such competition is highly political and can be settled only on a political level, that is by pressing and negotiating in all available ways, between ambassadors, prime minister and president, or cabinet members with similar responsibilities. A problem for Canada, of course, has been that what preoccupies a Canadian cabinet is often regarded as of peripheral importance in Washington. That is why the various ministerial committees have never worked. The American cabinet members could rarely be pinned down and adequately briefed for meetings with their Canadian counterparts, always brimming with interest, grievances, and statistics.

Differences over foreign policies have been important irritants, although the consequences have been less drastic than we often fear because Americans were rarely aware of what we are up to. Canadians assumed, for example, that Washington would react strongly against our withdrawal of some forces from Europe in the late sixties, but Congress hardly noticed. From time to time well-intentioned people suggested plans for better co-ordination of foreign policies. One specific commitment to consultation was attached to the NORAD agreement in 1957. It did assist somewhat in promoting military and diplomatic exchanges and for Canadians a somewhat better understanding of US assessments and intentions. The Cuban missiles crisis of 1962 made clear that there was no possibility of Canada's being consulted when the US was faced with a drastic emergency and had to decide in great secrecy what to do with forces largely its own. Exchanges have in fact taken place incessantly among diplomats and military men, on hot – or at least warm – wires and in such bodies as the PJBD or the inter-parliamentary group. For Canada there was much to be said for discussion in NATO or the UN where we could gain strength from coalitions, where American intelligence reports were diluted by those from other sources and we could contribute our own.

What we have needed most is to know about US policies before they jelled and went public, especially if there was some vital Canadian interest at stake – as for example over US policy on emplacement of anti-ballistic missiles near our border or designs for new aircraft. There seemed little alternative to the hard diplomatic slugging involved in knowing what the Yanks were up to. That has required a deployment of trained forces at the embassy in

Washington, including, of course, the specialist representatives of Canadian government departments, astute Congress-watchers, and large quantities of charm, persistence, and Canadian Club. Until recently Canadian governments were reluctant to lobby Congress intensively as doing so was contrary to our idea of good intergovernmental relations and the US administration would resent it. That position, as I shall describe later, has been made untenable by the inability of the US administration to make dependable agreements.

Our worldly wisdom has been that no mechanisms provide a valid alternative to the rough and tumble of diplomacy. It is worth noting that the diplomats themselves, who do the hard work and know the frustrations, are sceptical of promiscuous institution-building although they value the fact-finding or monitoring role that joint bodies can play and welcome any means of gaining the wandering attention of senators, officials, and editors. The professionals, though they cannot ignore the importance of good vibes, are wary of the love-feast at which the views of those very, very lovely people up north are listened to with passive courtesy and active applause and promptly mislaid in the Byzantine processes of American policy-extrusion.

3 / Rational Management

'Clearly, differences in approaches to foreign policy
here reach a point where rational management of a
crucial bilateral relationship may no longer be
possible.' MARK MACGUIGAN, 18 Oct. 1980[1]

So far, so good, one might say. Things could in theory be a
lot better but in practice a lot worse. Our informal relationship is possible, some scholars argue, because of a
common diplomatic culture. Are there, however, changing
factors which suggest that we can no longer with confidence leave our relations to a system which one might
call unstructured or perhaps chaotically webbed? What
is the value of 'a common diplomatic culture' if it is
increasingly hard-nosed? It is constantly said that we
are becoming more and more interdependent, but a
counter argument can be made that the trend is in the
other direction, that both governments are increasingly
nationalist. Canada is certainly displaying more muscle,
and the US might get its act together in retaliation. The
game between us seems now more like zero sum; one
man's gain seen as another man's loss.

The trend in the world at large is to a mood of restriction and protection. Our somewhat laissez-faire system
might serve well a time when both countries, especially
the larger, were confident enough to be generous, when
the US considered its role as bountiful. Americans are
more inclined now to see themselves as victims of their
own generosity to other countries and Canada as a rich

hoarder of resources and industrial competition rather than a junior partner deserving particular consideration in the mutual interest.

Another factor, one which threatens all international régimes, is the increasing inability of Western governments to govern, while necessity obliges them to direct their political economies much more actively than their antique philosophies admit. Canada confronts the obvious problem of composing national strategies in the face of regional diversities. The tactics of major industrial countries like Japan and France are driving other governments to manipulate their own economies in the struggle for markets. Our defence policies, for example, are intertwined with our industrial strategy.

We face not only competition with American industry but also an ideological confrontation with born-again free enterprise. We need to worry about the possible conflict between what our government feels required to do to sell reactors or uranium or control our own resources and the international regulations of GATT or OECD which we have promoted in the hope of controlling others. The resentment of the United States is likely to be particularly furious because in their eyes the long-standing Canadian tradition, both Liberal and Conservative, of governmental support of essential national services is socialistic, subversive, and unfair to free enterprising Americans. That such a policy has always been simple Canadian pragmatism to sustain life in an unequal relationship and is not applicable to a superpower is an argument few Americans can understand. The new hot gospellers in Washington, who disapprove of our misbehaviour, will, of course, be demanding that the government they want to get off their back climb on to ours. There is a real difference of philosophy here that has not mattered much when the mood was complaisant but which can turn nasty when either side gets ideological about it. Canadian economic nationalism is, in the view of Washington and some Canadians, ideological. The Canadian defence would be that it is simply a practical way to rectify a traditional imbalance which, if left unchecked, would deny us adequate control of our own economy.

The United States, we fear, is increasingly incapable of conducting rational relations with any foreign country as the federal administration, which alone is in a position to weigh all the factors, is bound and overruled by the captious actions of a Congress that is a law unto itself, disdainful even of international commitments. Herein lies the gravest cause for worry about the future of the Canada-US relationship. What is the use of rational negotiation of joint institutions with a US administration which cannot act on behalf of its country and which cannot determine what Congress will do? It matters to us also that the US has limited control of its own entrepreneurs but it must be acknowledged that the Americans make that complaint to Ottawa as well. This acclaimed system of government may well be beautiful as democratic theory, but for a country with which other countries have to live, it is self-indulgent. It is a system which, Americans tell us in answer to complaints, we ought to have got used to by now. So sacred is their constitution that not even the most liberal internationalists will admit its faults – with rare exceptions such as Lloyd Cutler who, in an article in *For-*

eign Affairs, recognizes that it is not only unfair to friends and allies but also bad for the United States. He cites as 'a particular shortcoming in need of a remedy ... the structural inability of our government to propose, legislate and administer a balanced program for governing.'[2] It greatly inhibits their capacity to fine-tune policies necessary to survive in a world in which they can no longer get their own way as easily as in the past. Cutler should know; he was the American negotiator of the east coast fishing agreements of two years ago that the Senate has declined to ratify – of which more later.

This is not just the old problem of having to kowtow to the whims of the US Senate as we have been instructed to do for years by US diplomats. The situation is very much worse since Watergate and Vietnam. Anxious to avoid responsibility for recent sins, the American people have concocted the comfortable theory that a wicked and secretive administration was responsible for corruption at home and the gross unwisdom of Vietnam. Congress, which had never seemed notably bold and moral in its attitudes to either of these tragic errors, is now to be the ultimate guardian of American good behaviour and national interest. The hands of the administration are tied so that it cannot, in its wisdom, make mutually beneficial trade treaties or strategic arms limitation agreements, cannot trade with or aid any country or even any international institution which acts in a way that does not please some pressure or regional group in the Senate. Considering itself above international law, it paralyses US policy on the supply of nuclear fuel or tuna fishing. It is what one former Canadian ambassador has called 'legislative imperialism.' Given recent Congressional vetoes and capricious addenda to treaties, Cutler points out that 'other nations now realize that our executive branch commitments are not as binding as theirs, that Congress may block any agreement at all, and that at the very least they must hold something back for a subsequent round of bargaining with the Congress.'[3]

It must be said, of course, that there are also more pardonable reasons for the greater assertion of legislatures in the US, in Canada, and elsewhere to control external policies. As William Diebold puts it: 'The United States faces a set of problems which can no longer be treated as if they were simply foreign policy problems and therefore in the province of the president; nor can matters be bridged with that splendid arrangement for delegated authority which made it possible to conduct an enlightened trade policy for about forty years. We are dealing here with matters that are domestic and international at the same time.'[4] Our Canadian foreign policy likewise now involves many more matters of intense interest to politicians, both federal and provincial, and the process of foreign policy-making in Ottawa has been drastically altered to meet this situation in the past decade or two. In our system of government, however, we can stand by the policies on which we are able to agree with foreign governments even if it gets more and more difficult to make up our own national mind.

This shift of practice threatens one of the essentials of the pragmatic Canada-US system I have been describing. So great is the need between our two countries for working arrangements on a thousand fronts, we cannot rely on treaties, which can take years to get through the US Senate. In the past we have had resort to executive agreements, memoranda of intent, exchanges of notes, or even, as in the case of the basic Ogdensburg agreement, a press release. These, however, are now largely proscribed by Congress. On matters as unimportant as Canadian relations, Congress does not act as a rational whole but as the endorser of the will of sectional clusters of senators and congressmen with a vested interest in their constituents' rights to fish or pollute. When Senator Pell said Canada should not have inflated a regional issue over fisheries into a national issue, Flora MacDonald rightly responded: 'We feel treaties between sovereign states are national issues ...'

One cannot even be sure, as in the case of the Garrison Dam, that senators will pay due attention to recommendations of the International Joint Commission, thereby undermining the credibility of one of our most valued bilateral institutions. The credibility of that honoured institution has in any case been diminished by the low priority the Reagan administration has accorded to appointing members and the months during which it has languished out of operation.

One case in particular has brought all this to a head, roused in our quiet diplomats something close to anger, and induced the Canadian ambassador and the secretary of state for external affairs to make unusually blunt speeches. It is the 1979 East Coast Fisheries and Maritime Boundary Treaties, made necessary by the extension of our economic zones 200 miles out to sea.[5] They were reached by negotiators after long and arduous argument.

64

Each side had to negotiate with its own pressure groups. There was no satisfying everyone, but eventually solemn agreements were signed, a sawoff of the kind civilized contestants recognize as essential. The US administration accepted them and recommended them to Congress. The Senate not only failed to ratify them; it barely condescended to look at them. The senators as a whole were uninterested, but they bowed to the will of the New England senators whose support they will need in their own sectional crusades. Eventually President Reagan withdrew them from the Senate.

Canadian exasperation is not so much over the substance of the agreements, which is not beyond valid criticism, but with the process. What must we do in such situations? Must we go through another set of negotiations with the US Senate, a mindless body with which one cannot deal? Should we be asked to make further concessions? If so, should we in future hold back a whole set of barter points for the second stage? If this is the way the US wants it, should we now move to what is being called a COD policy? Should we refuse to make any agreement with the US administration without assured delivery or at least signed pledges by the appropriate senators that they will support it? Senator Pell of Rhode Island had the effrontery to tell Canadians in Ottawa that it was up to us to make sure that any agreement we sign would have Senate support. Where does this lead? Aside from the fact that we, and other countries, are required to deploy forces which no country should be asked to exert in dealing with another, this is an intrusion into the policies of a foreign country which rouses bitterness and which we would certainly not permit in return. Can we no longer deal with each other as sovereign states, with the discipline of give and take?

These doubts in Ottawa about the word of the United States have affected the whole spectrum of our relations. An example was the insistence that we have not only the written promise of the president but also a joint resolution of Congress stating their intention to go ahead with the Alaska Pipe Line before we constructed the so-called prebuilt portion. We secured in August 1980 a ministerial memorandum of intent about acid rain, but the value of that from an outgoing administration was greeted sceptically and not accorded much respect by the new one. On a whole range of issues, from energy to the water quality of the Great Lakes, we need to deal with the US as an entity that can pledge itself to do things.

In most of our conflicts the resolution is much more important for Canada than for a giant conglomerate like the USA. Their own politics are their priority and, as in the case of Great Lakes water quality, even a well coordinated and well researched strategy on our part makes little headway against opposition too diffuse to counter.[6] As our under-secretary of state for external affairs has bluntly stated: 'The real issue of course is wider still. How do we manage our total relations with the USA – in all their economic, technical, environmental and political complexity – if we cannot manage the single problem of the East Coast Fisheries in spite of the special mechanisms and special efforts devoted to the matter on both sides.'[7]

We cannot, of course, pretend that our own lack of central governmental control is not a factor. Americans are quick to point out that Ottawa cannot always commit the provinces, although they usually have to go back to the early sixties for a significant example, when BC stymied for two years our ratification of the Columbia River Treaty. The Canadian government cannot easily, in response to US complaints, instruct the government of Saskatchewan over potash or the construction of an irrigation dam which might pollute Montana. There were times in the fisheries negotiations when Canada could not agree to American compromise proposals because of the intransigence of certain provinces. No democratic governments are omnipotent. They all have to plead to foreigners from time to time their inability to control the activities of their entrepreneurs, their media, or their law courts. It is only fair to quote the comment of a congressman when told that the Canadian government could not interfere with decisions of the Canadian Radio-Television and Telecommunications Commission: 'Are we going to be required to establish diplomatic relations with the CRTC in order to get this thing resolved?' What is different, however, is that in our form of government, when Ottawa has settled its internal conflicts and agreed with a foreign government on a policy, it has the power and the will to ratify it.

We should be a lot more aware of the virtues of our own form of government when there is a danger of our skidding into the American system. The men who worked out our kind of self-government sought solutions step by step for the problems that actually confronted them. There were too many philosophers involved in composing the US constitution. They turned out some lovely prose and a form of government that might just have served for a country with a large wall around it. Our constitution, written and unwritten, is well short of perfect, I need not add, but it is responsible government vis-à-vis foreign governments. For our own sakes we must continue to have the capacity to calculate rational policies towards the United States and negotiate with confidence. That is not intended as an argument for the centralization of power but rather for guarding jealously the ultimate responsibility of cabinet government. It is also a word of caution about schemes in which we would share decision-making with an unresponsible government.

If we are to continue a satisfactory life together on this continent, we must have ultimate confidence in rough justice. Whom do we turn to now? The State Department, where we have traditionally found understanding and concern for the totality of the relationship, is impotent. A strong president able to control Congress or even cast a veto on our behalf, as Eisenhower did, might help, although the trend to Congressional omnipotence is more than the consequence of weak presidencies. It seems to me that the United States is suffering, as are the rest of us in the Western world, from a new wave of well-intentioned but misguided populism which will not accord a priority to good government over pop government. When the Committee on Foreign Investment in the United States intervenes in the effort of a foreign company to take over an American company in the energy business, an official describes this as 'concern that a foreign government would be taking over a position in a sensitive industry.'[8] To whom in Washington can we point out that that is what has been worrying us for years and with

68

much greater cause? Whether or not the National Energy Policy is good for Canada is a legitimate subject for debate among Canadians, but the inability of Americans to see it in the perspective of Canadian history raises doubts about the possibility of an equitable régime.

Since the election of 1980 Americans have insisted that the Canadian reaction to the fate of the east coast fisheries calamity has been exaggerated, if not hysterical. We mistook, they say, the aberrations of a weak régime for a new course of US government. One can only hope they may be right, and in the early stages of a new régime, as one might expect, there are signs of stronger authority by the administration. There has even been a satisfactory move on one of our controversies over fish – west coast tuna. There remain nevertheless as constants the endless delays involved, the uncertainties of negotiation, and the need to deal with the United States at various levels. There remain also the need to educate every new administration about the Canadian connection and the historic fact that for about two out of every four years, as our kindly American friends warn us, we should not expect decisions on anything that might be electorally sensitive in Maine, North Dakota, or Oklahoma.

Perhaps we should bear in mind the strategy of General Brock who, in the light of our inferiority to the Yankee forces in 1812, advised, 'Speak loud and look big.' There was not much practical yield from all those valentines to Ken Taylor and the 'Take a Canadian to lunch' weeks across the States. We did put up a stubborn resistance on tuna, even to the point of arresting American poachers and insisting on a Senate commitment. Whatever the forms of our future relationship, we shall have to develop muscles, our bargaining power, our capacities to use prudently what we have to offer, and to increase where we can American dependence on us. We shall need steady nerves to stand firm, as in the case of the National Energy Policy, against the howls and threats from Congress and the *Wall Street Journal*. We need also to keep our calculators handy for we can never recklessly disregard the possible consequences of defiance. Standing up to the Yankees has never been a justifiable end in itself — except possibly at Queenston Heights.

One of our noteworthy successes was our defiance of US assertions in the Arctic by the Arctic Waters Pollution Prevention Act of 1970. It is worth noting because it was well disciplined action. We were able to do so because we were in situ, because we avoided direct confrontation and produced a new idea, a functional concept of pollution control zones for which coastal states would be responsible. It was a compromise but one which gave us what we needed without unnecessary defiance. It appealed also to other countries and led to the device of the economic zone which has been the most important product so far of the Law of the Sea Conference, adopted with enthusiasm by the United States which had hollered against our arrogant act. Power is not absolute but functional. It is a mistake to think of massive US military and economic power deployed against poor little Canada. On most issues there is a balance of the kind of strength applicable to the matter in hand.

So, in a ruthless age in which direction do we move? Will we be driven reluctantly into unitary structures, either general or specific, that promise to increase our prosperity or at least save us from bankruptcy, but make us junior partners in a continental company? The auto pact was an ad hoc experiment in this direction which avoided, however, the false principle of equality by including the device of safeguards for Canada. Whether it has been a success is a matter of dispute, although in assessing it one has to bear in mind that the alternative was probably not a flourishing Canadian automotive industry (flourishing about as much as that of Britain) but no automobile industry at all. This experiment has not been seen as applicable to other industries.

In considering what might be done it is advisable, in our pragmatic tradition, to look at new devices in terms of a rationalization of our needs rather than the ideology of free trade. If we have to go this way there is something to be said for entering with deliberate calculation into some broad junior partnership arrangement so that our energies would be directed towards strengthening rather than fighting the system. Our position in the eyes of the world would be clarified and we could act with the US as a recognized team. Perhaps we might call it sovereignty-association.

There are over twenty joint institutions now and within these channels has emerged, in the words of John Kirton, a 'diplomatic culture' in which 'emphasis is placed on working from a common data base, sharing information and proposals, focusing on the most advantageous technical solution to issues, insulating problems from the general climate of the relationship or disputes in other issue areas, and consciously seeking outcomes that provide bal-

71

anced and expansionary benefits.'[9] The weaker power has not heretofore dared to consign decision-making to a supra-sovereign body, no matter how fairly it is composed or how decent its intentions. It is virtually impossible for the interests of 230 million people to be equated with the interests of 24 million people in any council with power to decide. There is such a thing as a 'system's bias.'

This principle of jointness is one to be kept firmly in mind in considering the new schemes being presented to us. It is a principle Americans often find hard to understand because they believe in their own benevolence. Ronald Reagan was undoubtedly sincere when, as reported, he suggested that Canadian officials might at times attend US cabinet meetings, but he does not understand the consequences or implications of such a practice. We are not just being coy when we consistently decline invitations to have Canadian officials testify before lesser bodies, congressional committees and courts in the US. We cannot acquiesce in an American disposition, however generous, to treat us as if we were not really foreigners. To do so would commit us in some measure to policies in the making of which we would have had only a marginal voice.

We may want or be forced to look at new patterns going beyond the joint principle and be tempted by the prospect of sharing in the making of policies that affect us. We need not reject absolutely such experiments, but partial participation in continental policy-making is likely to prove so unsatisfactory that we would be obliged to press further, no longer able to turn back to restore our independence. In the eyes of the world, we would probably have lost that status already, forfeiting our right to act as an entity in international institutions of increasing importance to us.

If we contemplate continental devices, we must square them with our universal obligations or move farther towards a continental unit in order to get the kind of exemptions required for the likes of the European Community. In any case, the wider international agreements may not be adequate to the intense interpendence of the North American economies. Ottawa and Washington could find it necessary to make special deals on non-tariff barriers, about such controversial issues as government procurement, safeguards, or subsidies. Making such deals is not easy, however. One persistent problem is that the US forgets about us. It makes arrangements in GATT with the European Community or Japan in mind which bear harshly on Canada. It seems disposed also to use the GATT codes on non-tariff barriers not, as intended, to liberalize international trade, but to legitimize US laws and thus, in the words of Professor Lazar of York University, 'make it easier for US companies to bring forth complaints against almost any type of practice pursued by some foreign government.'[10] As far as Canada is concerned, the indications are that these practices would include all or any of those things we must do by way of an industrial strategy, including such essentials as government assistance to research and regional industry.

'If the multilateral arrangements do not work well,' the American scholar, William Diebold, has pointed out, 'then the question will arise whether Canada and the United States can afford to leave issues as unresolved as the

73

world as a whole or whether they will have to find better ways of working out their difficulties between themselves.' We would then, he adds, 'be facing a number of problems about how "special" the relationship between Canada and the United States was to be, whether seen in our eyes or those of the world, and whether to treat the relation as special would in some way help or hinder the growth of broader international agreements.'[11]

I still don't think we have reached that second last resort, and the American attitude to any request for sovereignty-association might be the same as Ottawa's. The problem is not one-sided. As Peter Towe, Canadian ambassador in Washington, said in October 1980, 'We are entering a period of co-operative independence through which runs a definite strain of what I would call "inter-vulnerability."' It is interesting to note, for example, that when the US secretary of commerce criticized Canada's foreign investment policy and hinted at seeking damages under GATT, he added his reservations: 'We have no evidence that unilateral U.S. government intervention in the international investment process would further the U.S. national interest. It could also prompt counteractions by other governments with adverse effects on the U.S. economy and U.S. foreign policy.'[12] In an interdependent world retaliation is not simple even for a superpower. When in July 1981 the securities sub-committee of the US Senate sought to punish Canada by obstructing take-overs of US companies by Canadian companies, they were abashed to discover that that was exactly what the Canadian minister of finance was trying to do himself in the interests of the Canadian dollar.

I hope we will not be driven to desperate measures by our lack of confidence, by the rhetoric of confrontational politics, by stereotyped bleatings from some elements of the business community, the strictures of our gloom-prone financial columnists, and the wails from those on the left who say that we are unredeemable. (I feel like suggesting to the wailers that, if the worst comes to the worst, we could always join Libya.) Without sharing the superstition that political integration would inevitably follow further economic collusion, I think we have to recognize that a national economy is part of a national culture. There are other paths to follow, closer to our long tradition.

When spouses take each other to court we can assume that the relationship is on shaky grounds. But is this necessarily true when two neighbours agree to adjudicate an intractable problem? The alternative may be to allow the dispute to fester or strong-arm tactics to come into play; to go to an international court may in fact be the civilized and neighbourly thing for two countries to do, as we have done on a number of occasions in our history back to Jay's Treaty. In recent times the notion seems to have fallen into disrepute although agreement was reached in 1979 to refer the Gulf of Maine maritime boundary dispute to third-party settlement. A joint committee of the Canadian and American Bars has recommended more frequent recourse to adjudication of legal disputes when all efforts at negotiation have failed and has proposed a treaty for this purpose. Canadians in particular should be prepared to look closely at mechanisms which would assure equality before the law.

Suggestions which build on the joint principle that has served us well have come recently from, among others, Maxwell Cohen,[13] former Canadian chairman of the IJC, and Rodney Grey,[14] our former negotiator in GATT. Another idea has been under consideration in the Canadian-American Committee, where the principal concern is over the conflicts arising as each country develops its own industrial strategy, now widely regarded as essential. These proposals vary; but the gist of them is an *advisory* body on economic conflicts the function of which would be essentially early warning and problem solving. Such bodies would be an extension of the formula of the IJC but not of the IJC itself. If we could get serious and responsible members, not just political hacks, opportunities would be provided for spotting conflicts of interest in advance and advising the two governments how to handle them. They would have to be taken seriously, for the value of the joint commissions depends critically on the quality of the members. Such mechanisms provide no obvious answer to the problem of the two-faced monster which is the US government or the eleven faces of Canada. They might help legislators as well as administrators to see more sides to an issue and raise their level of consciousness and conscience. On the other hand they could turn out to be continental planning bodies. In any case I cite these proposals not to endorse them but to indicate the directions in which I think we might most safely look for new institutions.

I wonder also if we might revive the practice of agreeing on certain principles as we did in the Statement of Principles for Economic Co-operation of 1950. Our defence production agreements, for example, have been based on a recognition that the political advantages for both countries of Canada's being a solvent ally require restraints on the brute force of economics. Might it be possible to get an understanding that for the lesser power there are legitimate cultural concerns – maintenance of healthy national media, for example – which cannot be determined by purely economic considerations and that the restriction of Canadian advertising in American journals and television is a defence of, not an assault on, the freedom of the press. Could we draw up rules of comity on anti-trust legislation, the extension of which by Americans to limit Canadian exports to China or Cuba has been a cause of persistent irritation?

Or did this kind of compact come more naturally in the sweeter fifties? Could one now hope to persuade the Senate to solemn agreement on principles which might run counter to their regional prejudices? Would they pay any attention to principles agreed to by the president alone? No doubt we would have to make pledges in return, possibly limiting our own rights to, for example, restrain American investment. The so-called Merchant-Heeney principles of 1965 were not very well received, but that was largely because they were misrepresented by the media and rarely read. The earlier agreements on principle were based on a frank recognition of inequality and the will of the stronger power to exercise restraint. Canada would always be unequal in gross product and population, but what if Canada, with its healthier equation of resources to population, should in due course become wealthier per capita – as seemed possible in the early seventies? What kind of attitude could we and should we expect from Americans towards that kind of inequality? Would the equitable sharing of energy resources be a principle on which the US would insist?

There is something to be said for and much to be said against the continental schemes which, as I mentioned earlier, are now being proposed from California and other fanciful environments. Whether or not we discover new forms for the continent, there is everything to be said for a closer study of the way the United States and Canada actually do deal with each other and ask ourselves with open minds if there are better ways. The ways could be simply habits and customs, agreements on process, or something going beyond the joint co-operative forms of the past.

The reality of the relationship, which is labyrinthine, has been obscured too long in indiscriminate metaphors of domination or equal partnership. Whatever it is, it is not equal, and we must never be seduced by a weakness for symmetry and sentimentality into designs which ignore inequality. To clear our minds it might be advisable to question the assumption that any joint mechanisms proposed are intended to integrate us more closely, whatever that means, or to continentalize and homogenize us. The media, both professional and amateur, unfailingly describe such proposals as projects for 'closer ties to the United States.'[15] The truth is, of course, that we are about as close together as we could possibly be. History and geography looked after that. We cannot disentangle ourselves or put up walls. Coping is inevitable. How to cope is the question, whether by vain efforts at isolation or by devising workable rules for the ménage. Canadians who are wary of 'closer ties' ought not to be frightened away from all talk about new institutions or arrangements on the assumption that the true North would necessarily become thereby less strong or less free. Their purpose in the past, as I have tried to illustrate, has often been to protect the Canadian interest in an unequal situation by ensconcing it.

Let me dispose first of all of the triangular concept which includes Mexico. It appeals to the Canadian instinct for counterweight, especially if, as is also being suggested, Jamaica and other islands could be brought in to dilute the omnipotence of the USA. Counterweight has been a sound instinct in the Canadian tradition when it bore some relation to reality, but the common ground on which one could base such a North American union, federal, confederal, or loose, seems to me chimerical. A certain fascination with the idea of 'continental unity' lingers from the fifties in spite of the dubious results in Europe. One should certainly not rule out specific, ad hoc regional agreements, even on energy, if all parties are willing and confident, provided, of course, they do not contravene our commitments to GATT or other international disciplines which link the continents. How, for example, would we square this trilateral energy accord with our obligations to the International Energy Agency? There are arguments for strengthening mutually beneficial links between Canada and Mexico, but not for entwining these in the serious and quite different problems between the United States and Mexico. It is hard to understand, furthermore, why Mexico would be interested. As for

Canada, Mark MacGuigan told an American audience recently that 'our relationship with the United States is too complex and rich to fit easily into an artificial "conceptual framework" more suited to the classroom than to the real world.'[16]

We need good but not grandiose conceptions. We still suffer from those postwar assumptions that the world was destined to find prosperity and security in a federation of large continental unions. These were attributable to the rather un-Canadian illusion that federalism is an automatic dissolver of conflict and to a worship of global efficiency in the abstract that is now being countered by a healthy vigilence towards big and multilayered government. The threat to the European Community of sheer unwieldiness is a lesson for others. We must constantly be wary of the innate tendency of the businesslike Americans to assume that the most efficient running of the continent is the highest good. We are more aware now that economies of scale become tyrannies of scale.

In spite of their weakness for grandiose designs, Americans of late have been more nationalistic than imperialistic. They may, for understandable reasons, cast covetous eyes on the resources of their neighbours but their mood a century after the acquisition of Alaska would be more sceptical of a manifest destiny to become trilingual or to expand the bureaucracy of Washington to administer a whole, vast continent. Along with Hibernia they would get Mr Peckford, and with hydro power and asbestos comes M. Lévesque. Now that governments have become infinitely more responsible for the welfare of their peoples, the imperial perspectives of the nineteenth and early twen-

80

tieth centuries have altered. One might recall the wise comment of Lord Bryce to Professor G.M. Wrong of Toronto: 'If Canada did not exist it would be in the interest of the United States to create her.'

This is not to say, however, that the relationship among the North American countries is fixed for all time. There is something to be said for more or less regular meetings between the heads of government or other ministers of Canada, the United States, and Mexico, although we must be wary of the American inclination to regard such sessions as briefings. Has it occurred to the proposers in Washington of this trilateral accord that deference would be due to the Mexican view on El Salvador, for example?

Canadians have remained somewhat sceptical since the first such meeting at White Sulphur Springs in 1956 of the two presidents and a prime minister. The barely concealed purpose of that séance was to show the American electorate that President Eisenhower was fit for re-election after his coronary attack by exposing him to the two foreign leaders least likely to put a strain on his heart. As one who accompanied a very sceptical Mr St Laurent on that expedition I can testify that it was all heart, with a certain amount of briefing and a limited expectation of reply, but nevertheless a forum which could be useful if we could establish a precedent for listening all round. As Adlai Stevenson once said, the technological instrument Americans most need is a hearing-aid.

Just as we need a constructive attitude to the re-shaping of our own confederation, we can regard the evolution of the continent as a continuing experiment. We have been beguiled too long with the illusions and spectres of

81

absolute positions – utter independence or total assimilation. What the world needs from us is proof that weak and strong countries can adjust in order to co-exist satisfactorily. With open minds towards new 'conceptual frameworks,' however, we need not close them to the possibility that the more traditional relationship, subject always to adjustment, may be if not the best of all possible worlds at least better than the world we don't know. At a recent conference on the future of the International Joint Commission the homely wisdom of an artisan was cited: 'If it's working, don't fix it.'

4 / On Being an Ally

'... thou hast great allies
Thy friends are exultations, agonies.'
WILLIAM WORDSWORTH, *To Toussaint L'Ouverture*

As a result of our eccentric past we don't think in all things like Americans even if we chew the same gum. This is especially true in foreign policy. I would like now to consider that cloudy prospect before us to illustrate the importance of rational differentiation – a principle I would say of functionalism if I dare use that word again. We have had considerable experience of difference with American foreign policy, rarely at 90 degrees but often at 45, more often about means than ends. In the world at large we are now passing from an era in which alignments and loyalties were simpler. It is likely to be a harsher and less tolerant period. If we are to work, as we must, alongside our formidable friend and neighbour and keep our own faith, we shall require steady nerves, mature patience, and a firm grasp of principles. A point for Canadians always to bear in mind is that the differences in our approaches to foreign policy are attributable not only to our national experiences but also to the very great difference in the consequences to the world of what our two countries do.

The variation in our perspectives on the society of nations may be illustrated by our attitudes to coalitions. Frank Underhill, who preferred on the whole to stress North American common causes, told an American audience of his conviction 'that we Canadians have a great deal more experience than you Americans have in working this loose international system of concurrent majorities.'[1] Americans are prejudiced in favour of majority action; we have preferred consensus. In the Commonwealth, for example, there is no voting and the commitment is to consultation rather than unanimity. In the Organization of American States, there is provision for majority decision and minority obedience, one of the reasons we have never joined. In NATO, in the shaping of which we played some part, there is no voting, although the greater responsibility of the larger powers is conceded in practice. Lesser powers are faced with the need to act along with allies and associates with much less hope of determining the common policy but no intention of surrendering to others their right to determine their own actions.

The Canadian way, after the learning experience of the Commonwealth, is to deny logic in the interest of doing whatever is possible. The great power, confident that Mother knows best, is slow even to recognize that there is a problem. On the other hand, it must be said, the smaller power can too easily fail to remember the extent to which the common cause is his own and not just that of the domineering powers. Our record since the last war of balancing a common international interest against domestic pressures has on the whole been good, although the public and politicians often find the juggling hard to tolerate. Our American friends sincerely profess their respect in principle for some nonconformity of allies but find a human difficulty in accepting it when it is actually practised.

Our experience should prove valuable because the art of alliancemanship is what we shall need most. Two of the specific problems we face are the urgent need for the United States to learn better how to be an ally and our own need – all the greater in present circumstances – to act in association with others if we are to have any influence on the United States. If we slip into regarding ourselves primarily as two associated North American states, then I think we are faced with frustration and impotence, as well as confused and angry arguments about loyalty. In that kind of harness we are bound to be the wagged tail.

The basic requirement for better alliance behaviour is respect for the other's responsibilities, intelligence, and good faith. It is folly for us to expect the Americans to pay as much attention to our views as we must pay to theirs. Nevertheless, Canadians might bear in mind that our foreign policies became less divergent in the seventies – not because we were forced to conform but rather because the US moved towards our positions on such controversial subjects as China, Cuba, Vietnam, and détente. Our example was certainly not what moved them, although in the case of China it was a catalytic factor. The convergence cannot be attributed to structural causes – better means for consultation and co-ordination. There was no striking of bargains over foreign policy for domestic advantage, a ploy dear to the heart of abstractionist critics and so far from the real world. It was not achieved by our making speeches at them. There are no simple formulas or mechanisms. Awareness is all. As we expect American sensitivity to our foibles, so too we must recognize their tender spots. In calculating how to cope with the USA we might be guided by that Benedictine prescription: 'so to temper all things that the strong may still have something to long after, and that the weak may not draw back in alarm.'

Since we swam out into the world scene with a bolder stroke some forty years ago we have, as I have been arguing, learned a good deal about the tactics, postures, and policies of lesser powers in general and ourselves in particular. Two lessons from these experiences I would like to repeat and stress. First is the essentiality for us of international institutions. They create the fabric of a world in which we could survive and prosper and provide the best possible way to exercise some influence on events and some control over our great ally and leader. The other lesson is the requirement for a lesser power of an adaptive and responsive foreign policy, based not on an abdication of our own will but a recognition that the world will lurch in directions unforeseeable which we may or may not like. We must not be stuck with one of those neat and all-encompassing foreign policies so beloved by political scientists, editors, and members of the opposition (regardless of party) designed only for a foreseeable future. A sense of direction we need, an outline of goals to be sought, alternative scenarios, a grasp of forces at work in all parts of the world so that we can make up our minds swiftly. But when the United States or our other allies – over Vietnam or Suez or the neutron bomb – do things we have argued against, we cannot simply say 'Stop the World. I want to get off.' We have to cope with new situations not of our making but from which we cannot isolate ourselves. We are not obliged to accept with a docile smile President Reagan's and Mr Haig's view of the world, but we had better adjust our calculations and our hopes to a new set of facts. We can disagree with the United States but not reject it.

Wider international institutions do not, of course, provide all the answers. There is still the specialness of propinquity. In chapters 2 and 3 I looked at the bilateral relationship, the need to deal on a special basis with economic, defence, and territorial questions even within the context of multilateral agreements. This close association may at times require us to take a common stand, or rather coincidental stands to the wider world. It is a reason for the Americans to cultivate our support. On some issues, the sale of reactors, uranium, or wheat, for example, or Northern strategy, our influence will be considerable on functionalist grounds. In general questions of foreign policy, however, we must not be tempted by the illusion that there is an institution or a formula of consultation that would give us a North American foreign policy, or the promise of what might be called an equitable share in the US policy process. I would not put it past our new generation of whiz kids to produce a computer that would accord Canada, on our own rep by pop principle, one-tenth of a common voice – just enough to get us involved in every US adventure or screw up every decision by Washington on which the peace of the world might depend.

I would not want to give the impression that the United States is the cause of the dangers ahead of us, although in any world problem it is a major player. The precarious stability maintained in most of the world since the last war is threatened by events in Eastern Europe, Southeast Asia, Africa, and Latin America. The situation is rendered more dangerous by the declining power, in all things other than arms, of both superpowers and the consequent weakening of their nerves and their capacity to manage the scene. The East-West confrontation remains, and it is complicated by the various confrontations of North and South. These changes are by no means all bad, even if they are disconcerting. They hold out the prospect of a more equitable ordering of the world balance if we can rise to the challenge. The economic and security interests of Canada are more deeply engaged than ever before. Aloofness is not for us a possible alternative, however deep our desire to be left alone and immaculately independent. If less can be expected of the United States, more will be required of the rest of us.

The problems face us regardless of the change of régime in Washington, but they are complicated by the uncertainties about directions in which the new administration will move. There is, of course, no capital in the world which is not watching closely, and it is well to remember that Washington, in its unwisdom, is going to be more concerned about the reactions of capitals other than Ottawa. It is possible that the new régime may, as they have suggested, assign a higher priority to Canada. That is no doubt as it should be, but it is also worrying. If their views vary considerably from what one might roughly call the Canadian consensus, or at least the views proclaimed by the government we have elected, we might be more comfortable out of the limelight.

Differences with the Americans over foreign policy, as I see it, are as likely to divide as to unite the Canadian people. Oppositions, regardless of party, will accuse the government of being either too pro- or too anti-American, disregarding too often the intrinsic merits of each issue. The power of the United States media is such that it can affect the Canadian consensus. The problem is not that Canadians become converted to the official American view; they are bombarded by too many opposing American viewpoints. It is rather that they identify themselves with the American debate and lose their Canadian perspective. Their hold on the pronoun 'we' is fitful. It is perfectly right and proper that many Canadians should on important issues agree with American policy and argue the same route for Canada. It is less sound, however, when they lose their awareness of Canadian policy or argue simple conformity to the views of an avuncular protector and benefactor. It is even more foolish to insist on simple opposition to prove our manhood. This failure is detectable on the left as well as the right. We have had the spectacle of ardent anti-Americans in Canada identifying themselves almost totally with the United States action in Vietnam which they deplored. Some begrudge the Americans exclusive right to their sins. I recall a cartoon of a decade ago depicting a band of Canadian protestors on Parliament Hill bearing placards: 'The Canadian government is unfair. We want a draft to dodge.' This kind of alienation contributes to a dilution of concern by Canadians for Canadian policy which is, after all, the instrument by which we can hope to influence events.

Americans, unable to comprehend why Canadians might want to own more of their energy industry, are quick with conventional theories which don't apply. Even a reasonably well-informed group of Americans in a study by the Atlantic Council of the United States saw in the National Energy Policy an effort on the part of the Canadian government to heal its internal wounds by conjuring up a foreign enemy. A policy such as the NEP does have as a consequence the provocation of antagonism in the US which, by its unreasonableness, could increase support for the policy. The Americans should not, however, be allowed to get away with this self-serving delusion. The idea that the NEP unites Canadians would, in any case, be seen as ludicrous by observers who fix their eyes on the realities of Canadian political and economic life.

The international problems that face President Reagan and his advisers and the United States Senate are staggering. We must make clear that we understand sympathetically what a very difficult thing it is to be an American if we expect them to listen to us. We cannot afford flippant disagreement. There are aspects of the new administration's attitude towards Central America which many of us have found disquieting. Before we oversimplify the complex issues in El Salvador in slogans, however, we should ponder precisely what any outside power can and should do in a situation so bloody that justice is almost impossible to establish. The assignment of guilt is in itself no solution. There have been indications of US opinion on other foreign affairs that are equally disturbing, their attitudes to the United Nations, for example, but it is not only fair but wise to save our sharper contradictions until the new men have settled into the responsibilities of office. New governments always have to find out that the world is round and that a government's freedom of action is more constricted than those in opposition assume. Brusque confrontation may only entrench a new government more stubbornly in its preconceptions. On our part a willingness to listen need not appear as the silence that implies assent. The sober restatement of our own views can forestall sharp rebuke later. It is of very great importance to Canada to maintain amicable relations with whatever administration the Americans elect. That does not mean supine agreement, but it suggests caution in picking a quarrel. The danger is that we forfeit not only our vested interests but also the disposition in Washington to listen to our arguments on world affairs.

Certain aspects of the challenge are already apparent. President Reagan is cutting foreign aid, even though the American contribution has been declining for a decade. The Canadian government is in the forefront of the campaign for a new economic relationship with the developing world. A clash of philosophies on this subject may be expected. Our stance will be strong only if we are seen to be practising what we preach. What reputation we have on the international circuit depends on the reputation we have acquired as reliable practisers rather than vacuous preachers.

It is clear that the new administration will expect its allies, especially Canada, to follow its own lead by increasing defence expenditures. If we resist, we shall not get much support from our other NATO allies, most of whom also think we are dragging our feet. Our voice in NATO councils could inevitably be diminished at a time when those bodies become of greater importance to us as the most likely means of control over United States strategic policy and of differing with them, if need be, in company. On the other hand, there are so many contradictions to be faced in forming a rational defence policy for the second broadest country on earth and so many domestic reasons for using the money otherwise that the decision to go ahead on anything like the American scale is forbidding.

We could consider a declared policy of shifting our role in world security to the economic front, arguing that we can play there a more useful and effective part and one more appropriate to our kind of power than as a fifth wheel in Western defence. That argument, to be convincing, would have to be sustained, of course, by massive commitments to foreign aid matching the astronomical price of aircraft and tanks. What is more, the commitment cannot be fulfilled simply by handing out large sums; it would mean drastic revision of our commercial and financial policies and taking sides in UN debates on the New International Economic Order that offend our allies, not to mention many of our own voters. If we relieved ourselves of the burden of defence expenditures, I fear also that the United States Congress would regard this as an artificial means of spurring our competitive position in trade and would insist on more non-tariff barriers to our exports.

If I am constructing a maze, I am doing so deliberately. There is no glib way out of this puzzle. I am not arguing here the virtues of any of these courses but simply pointing out that one way or another we have to share more responsibility and pay up – and probably irk our good neighbours whatever we do.

There are various reasons to fear that the Weltanschauung from Washington will not be in harmony with that from Ottawa or from Bonn or Brussels or Mexico City. Our interest is in promoting as much consensus as possible without abandoning our self-respect. In NATO we are cast as odd man out by the pretence of the European members to have a common policy. The fact that they do not have a common policy on any major issue only adds confusion and friction. If we are to avoid harsh exposure to the Americans as a dissident and, what is more important, if we are to have any influence at all on policy, we shall do our best work as the patchers-up of Atlantic compromises. We can do this more readily because there is no European and no North American view as conventionally suggested. Our Weltanschauung is closer to that of the Germans, Dutch, and Italians while the British are at one with the Americans. We serve not only our own interests but those of the alliance in working against the increasing tendency to bipolarize it as 'Europe' and 'America.'

I would certainly not rule out positions of loud non-conformity when there seems no honourable alternative and if we are sure of our ground, but let us not pretend that life with an angry uncle would be easy. It would be considerably more comfortable to differ with the Americans in company with the Europeans, or at least some of them. That is the strong argument for working not independently but through the alliance on matters of grand strategy. In so doing we would not avoid Washington's wrath, but our offence would seem less rank.

In suggesting a prudent caution about Washington's wrath I am not reviving discredited theories about economic retaliation. I am simply arguing that life is a good deal more comfortable for Canadians if there is at least a minimum of good will across the border. It is important to our material well being that we be regarded by Congress and the administration as a good ally, although we should never allow ourselves to be blackmailed or bought. It is not an easy position to be in, and it will be no easier as the game gets rougher. That is why I risk contumely by arguing that our first priority should be the seeking of compromise, that old smoothie role so much deplored in recent years.

I am not proposing any abstract role of mediation but an approach based on a careful calculation of the short- and long-term interests of Canada on and off this continent. It is our traditional assignment in NATO. Alienation and contention within the alliance are not in our national interest. As the shape of the North Atlantic triangle has been skewed in the past few years and we have been hypnotized into seeing ourselves too exclusively as North Americans, we have been losing sight of what for a century was the fundamental priority in our foreign policy – to prevent the British and the Americans and later the West Europeans and the Americans from falling out. The expectations of what we can accomplish on our own must, of course, be restrained to avoid discouragement, a state of mind we so perversely enjoy.

There are certain as yet unresolved ambiguities in the Washington outlook as I see it. The apparent anxiety to restore US power and influence as it once was does not accord very well with the assessment of the friendly allies: that the US must accept a role that is still unique but somewhat more like that of an ordinary state. It is not that we are eager to cut the Americans down to size but we don't want them to make any more disastrous miscalculations of their capacity, as in Vietnam. This means in particular that the United States must be more willing to act through international institutions and alliances, with more respect for the principle of concurrent majorities. Above all it must not, as in the case of Afghanistan, announce unilaterally the sanctions to be taken and make the conformity of its allies a test of loyalty. It is not healthy for the US that Canadians and others should be put in the position of taking actions against the Soviet Union 'to support the United States,' as it was put to us. The Soviet offence was against us all, and the sanctions should have appeared as the expression of a common will. That could only be possible if there was agreement in advance on the kinds of sanctions that might be effective. The Americans defend their actions on the grounds that someone has to act when the allies can't agree. It is in some cases a legitimate argument, but it can, of course, mean that the allies won't agree with the will of Washington. In any case the allies have to be given a chance to agree before some White House spokesman announces what they are expected to agree on.

Somehow we have to convince the new American leaders that our anxiety that they become better allies and not act unilaterally is inspired by concern for their own interests. They can still expect great forbearance from friends and allies and clients because of our concern for the preservation of their strength and their reputation, but the Europeans are not going to accept without question their policies on détente or the Middle East, and the Latin Americans are not going to accept without question their unilateral policies in Central America. Where we must stand especially firm is in upholding the UN system and the sacred principle of international institutions, without which we cannot exist, against the challenge of the innocents in Washington.

The most frightening portent of a new American policy is the rude intervention in the Law of the Sea Conference as it was on the point of winding up its extraordinary endeavour over many years to establish an equitable maritime system. The new régime said they wanted to reconsider their commitments and fired their negotiators as if they had been traitors. The apparent rejection of this great multilateral compromise in response to greedy internal pressures is especially alarming because UNCLOS has proved, more successfully than any other UN endeavour, that ways and means can be invented for successful multilateral diplomacy, the greatest need of mankind in this age of interdependence. There is a beguiling reasonableness in Washington's request for a longer opportunity to look at texts with which they are unfamiliar and their explanation that it is better to warn now than have the other parties disappointed by a later rejection by Congress. This, however, is not a renegotiated bilateral treaty. It is a compact with some 150 other countries, all of whom are asked to wait upon the whim of one party. What is more, we have again the unstated assumption that the US Senate acts on a plane above the law of nations. As the Canadian secretary of state for external affairs, Mark MacGuigan, put it recently: '... there is an instinctive view among many U.S. policy-makers and negotiators that international law should conform with U.S. law, rather than the other way around. Thus too U.S. negotiators often seem to expect the representatives of other countries to give the same automatic deference as they do to the procedural and institutional peculiarities of the U.S. system.'[2] Such was our anxiety to keep the US Senate happy in the system that we let them get away with habits that are not so easily tolerated now when US strength and importance have diminished.

How can there be successful international negotiation of this complexity if the representatives of the world's strongest country cannot be held to their bargains? It is the same problem, writ large, that we face over the east coast fisheries. It is behaviour by the United States which the rest of the world is less and less disposed to tolerate as that country is less and less the world's benefactor. One can easily imagine the attitude of US senators if the rest of us were to adopt their exalted form of democracy and insist on negotiating in their evasive manner. We can only hope that the new men in Washington will, if given a chance, see the consequences of their action over the Law of the Sea for the world order they cherish. For that reason coaxing and persuading are for the moment wiser tactics than denunciation. We must try to avert a betrayal as tragic as the Senate's rejection of the League of Nations. It is essential to let the president and his advisers know that his good friends among others regard a withdrawal from the new Law of the Sea as unacceptable – an adjective of which they seem particularly fond. In our anger, however, it is wise to realize that we as well as the United States are getting more than our fair share of the seas' resources from the LOS bargains as they now stand. We have a genuine concern with this threat to the future of international law but our highly respected contribution to this great international venture has been tarnished by the greed of our claims.

The new men seem to place a good deal of emphasis on strengthening the alliance. Alexander Haig is a staunch NATO man. That emphasis is largely associated with a determination to share more equitably the military burden. Sharing the policy-making seems less on their minds. It is, of course, a chicken and egg matter. The inequality of the military effort justifies the US tendency to unilateralism, whereas the incautious commitments of the United States, particularly those outside the NATO area, discourage the sense of responsibility for the alliance on the part of the rest of us. Can we in Canada remain aloof from the problems of the Persian Gulf, the Indian Ocean, or Central America which Washington regards as critical and which we on our own recognize as dangerously affecting the world order on which we depend?

The question of NATO action, or at least NATO attitudes, on issues outside the originally prescribed NATO area now becomes more of a problem. From the beginning Canada has maintained that the area of NATO responsibilities should be strictly limited. We have insisted that any involvement on our part in distant quarrels must be in accordance with United Nations action. Initially our concern was over commitments to our European allies who still had their colonial possessions, but that is now a minor problem. Later we have been more anxious to avoid involvement in American military or para-military enterprises in Latin America, the Middle East, Southeast Asia, or, for example, French interventions in Africa. Unlike the Australians and New Zealanders we never sent fighting forces to Vietnam. It would be unwise to rule out fighting along side the Americans in some honourable cause of which we, in our own judgment, approve, but whatever the enterprise our position would be awkward. It would be most awkward in situations in which we agree with American policy. If there is not support in NATO or the UN for the American cause, we could be in an exposed position indeed.

One of our reasons for joining NATO was to avoid this dilemma. Partnership with the US in continental defence is one thing, being a small part of an expedition abroad over which we could expect little control is another. What the Americans seem to want in the Middle East is not that the allies join their proposed rapid deployment force but that they send forces of their own in parallel gestures. But what conceivable contribution of that kind could a country Canada's size make on its own? In Korea Canadians fought alongside the Americans but in a Commonwealth Brigade within a UN Command. Our obvious way out is to continue to say that we will take part only in military action blessed by the UN, but that admirable position can appear hypocritical when we know that in the Middle East and elsewhere there is no veto-free majority forthcoming for the kinds of expeditions that might seem necessary to the Americans, our other allies, and to us. One possible way of playing our part would be to increase our contributions to NATO to relieve those great powers who might feel required to deploy forces elsewhere. There is no easy, let alone tidy, solution to this inevitable quandary of a lesser power in a very wide and very turbulent world.

There is another theme detectable in the Reagan foreign policy fugue and that is Fortress America. A mighty fortress is our continent! The note is militant but as yet in the background. Americans are adjured to stop regarding Mexicans and Canadians as foreigners (although we have both been struggling for centuries to maintain that status) and to ponder a North American accord dependent largely on our own resources in God's continent. It would be unwise to leap to conclusions as to what this means and whether the theme will recur at all, but it is prudent to note an apparent last-ditch isolationism lurking in the background. If the Third World remains perversely hostile and the Europeans and Japanese perversely selfish, then we three – or more probably two – fall back on Fortress America. It is unlikely that the Mexicans would want to enter the fortress, except as a very last resort. Some Canadians will be tempted by the promise of security and the apparent rewards. We thought of things like this in the black summer of 1940, and no one would rule it out if the worst was coming to the worst.

Well short of that drastic consideration, however, is a situation that could soon emerge. If the NATO community becomes more like a dumbbell, we are tacitly prescribed a part on a North American team. We might hope

for special attention as a special ally, even to the extent of
better deals on automobiles or fish. Surely it would then
be churlish to squawk about El Salvador or fail to consider some kind of assistance to the Middle East. In the
eyes of many Europeans, especially the French, we are
already just a smaller North American echo. That is why
the French did not want our prime minister at the Summit. At the Summit there are many issues on which we do
see eye to eye with the Americans and we must say so.
Nevertheless, we could fear the day when we had become
so infected with the North American syndrome, when we
got all our ideas from the *Wall Street Journal*, that the
Canadian prime minister would appear at those high-class
summits more like the president's pet poodle. (I am envi-
sioning, needless to say, some future prime minister.)
Before succumbing to the promise of a place on an all-
North American team we should bear in mind also that
the Senate does not give the US administration the power
to reward allies for loyalty or even to make a guaranteed
deal and that their form of government makes this kind of
partnership a very dubious proposition.

I return to my contention that the inequality is such
there is no safe basis for partnership that cannot be very
carefully defined and staked out. In our defence policy we
have found ways of conducting joint continental defence
with safeguards and allocated responsibilities. In the
same pattern we can envisage régimes for the better
ordering of the economy of the continent although they
are not easy to work out. In matters of foreign policy,
however, there is no escape from the constant calculation
by a sovereign government in Ottawa of how to balance

our own attitudes and interests with the deference we owe to those of our major ally and co-defender of our vast territory. Foreign policy is the sum total of some thousand items, on many of which we have little in common with the USA. The commitment of an ally, as set out in Article 2 of NATO, is to take into consideration other allies' interests before differing. It is hard to find formulas that take us beyond that general principle.

In stirring times a call for prudence in our foreign policy is not popular. Hot-blooded journalists constantly reject it as typical Canadian gutlessness. But too much is stirring in these times. There are too many explosions about to be set off. What we want most is prudence in Washington, prudence in Moscow, not to mention prudence in Teheran. Our advice to be careful is not likely to be more effective if we holler it recklessly.

Alliancemanship is, of course, not enough. We shall be more effective and more comfortable if we lift our eyes beyond our shores and redouble our efforts to make universal and in some cases regional international institutions work. From Korea to Vietnam and southern Africa we have found that we have more influence as part of a larger team. For many of our diverse interests, and particularly relations with the Third World, the Commonwealth serves our purpose well. Since the assembled Commonwealth was able to turn certain tragedy into hope for Zimbabwe we trust the Americans will regard its efficacy a little more seriously than they have in the past. No one association serves all our needs. We must listen to the Asians. In the fifties when there was sharp division in the West over China, we listened to the advice of the Indians and tried hard, with some success, to keep Washington and Delhi from confrontation. It would seem to me wise to see if we might co-ordinate our stance on Central American crises with the Mexicans and Venezuelans. So much the better if the Americans join in. We were wise, like the Mexicans and Venezuelans, to be cautious about President Reagan's intentions in inviting the three countries to talk in Nassau in July 1981 about an aid programme in the Caribbean, but so long as he seems disposed to listen to other views, we ought not to take a churlish position.

Above all we must seek to persuade our friends in Washington and London from their shallow assessments of the United Nations system. The United States, in particular, will do itself and all of us great harm if it misjudges fleeting majorities in UN bodies and concludes that the system is hostile. A vigorous presentation of the American case in the face of unfair rhetoric and resisting hostile majorities is certainly called for, but a posture of denigrating and fighting the UN as an institution would only stimulate on an infinitely more dangerous scale the kind of rabid anti-Americanism of which we have only glimpsed the ugly face in Iran. It is an anarchical force which bodes no good for the First, Second, or Third Worlds. Our interest is in keeping criticism of the US rational. We and our friends have enough trouble now coping with the very rational resentments swelling in the UN towards the actions of the new US régime and its permanent representative. The circle is vicious, for the manifestations of that resentment serve to confirm the view from Washington that the UN is anti-American. By arguing that we must work constructively within the UN to gain our ends rather than reject it we reiterate a point of view which, in one context or another, we have been putting to the Americans, alone and in company, for over thirty years.

5/Canada's Roots

If there is a central theme in these essays it is that life with Uncle Sam will always be strenuous but that it can be reasonably comfortable and profitable if we take it calmly and pragmatically. Now I propose to take a very personal look at our roots, the history that has made us different, searching for our national genius to clarify our present sense of direction and calm our nerves. I shall, of course, shamelessly seek evidence for the arguments I have already made.

One such conclusion is that grand schemes for the continent are to be avoided. We can leave those to the Americans to whom they come more naturally. We, of course, have indulged in fantastic schemes ourselves such as the Dominion of Canada from sea to sea, not to mention New France from Quebec to Louisiana, but our ambitions were not pan-continental. It is the Americans who have nourished a mission of redemption for North America at large. Fortunately they don't think of us often enough to push their grand schemes *à l'outrance*, from Manifest Destiny to a North American accord. There is a strong conscience that restrains them from forcing their will on us – a discrimination in our favour in which one might detect (if one considers, for example, what happened to the Mexicans) some racial bias.

Canadians have constructed out of long experience and in response to felt needs structures which have served us pretty well. Great caution has been exercised over schemes which prescribe a North American entity because the facts of population and resources are such that the life we Canadians have built for ourselves over three centuries would soon be drained out of us. Like every other country we have restricted our freedom of action by thousands of agreements in the mutual interest but retained the ultimate sovereignty of our government.

To insist on safeguards and on differentiation is not to be anti-American, although it may run counter to the pop philosophies of homogenization and one-worldism. Our structures have evolved through a state of hot war to cold war to 'peaceful and harmonious co-existence' – well, more or less. Our triumph, for which the more powerful country deserves especial credit, has been the gradual establishment of a civilized relationship based on process and habit rather than on supranational institutions. The argument for differentiation in the present era is not ancestral animosity but the need for diversity in modern life and the staggering impossibility of running this ungainly continent from one capital. It may be significant that the one time in four centuries we were united under one sovereignty, from 1763 to 1776 or thereabouts, the British wallowed so hopelessly in the continental paradoxes that they set off the American Revolution.

Because we have no North American constitution we are saved from the agonies of patriating or matriating it. Nevertheless, the forms require our constant attention because circumstances change. What we need, however, are unagonizing reappraisals, reconsideration as an unending process. We need a better appreciation of the flexible system within which we work. We Canadians need a great deal more self-confidence, confidence in our past, present, and future, a calmer assumption that Canada is here to stay and that it is, all things being considered, a good thing. Changes of government on either side can pose new challenges, but the range of new choices is limited by geography, history, and a kind of unwritten constitution, based on habits and expectations.

In the earlier chapters I have sought to define the persistent paradoxes of life with a superpower. We find security in the Americans' power and insecurity in considering what wild things they might do with it. Access to their great store of finance, culture, and customers helps us prosper, while it aggravates our vulnerability. We maintain, because we must, faith in the liberal, democratic principles which inspire the Great Republic, but the raucous cries of the super-patriot and the missionary keep us on edge. My argument in general has been that these contradictions cannot be resolved. The beginning of wisdom is to live with them. They add zest to life with Uncle Sam, and save us from torpor. There is no solution for Canadian-American relations, and, I fear, no end of lectures on the subject. Coping with the fact of the USA is and always has been an essential ingredient of being

Canadian. It has formed us just as being an island formed Britain.

It is well to recall, in our sullen moods, that living beside a giant was a life's work chosen by our own forefathers. It was not thrust upon us by the Americans who, after all, had no good reason for wanting Canada to exist. It was not forced upon us by the British either, who had little enthusiasm for saving us from the Republic. The United States owes us nothing – except the application of those principles of good international behaviour enshrined in their Declaration of Independence and the United Nations Charter.

Living and coping with paradox is one of the things Canadians do rather well, better perhaps than our more decisive neighbours. The trouble is that we don't always recognize the dialectical approach as a merit. The roots of this instinct have been traced by Northrop Frye to the Quebec Act which was, in his words, 'an inductive, pragmatic recognition of a de facto situation, and the situation was one of those profoundly illogical ones that Burke considered typical of human life generally. The two factors to be taken into account were: (a) the British have conquered the French (b) the British have done nothing of the kind. The only way out of this was a settlement that guaranteed some rights to both parties.'[1]

And so we were launched in a framework designed to protect the citizen from the tyranny of general principles. We sought from our authorities 'peace, order and good government' rather than such personal goals as 'life, liberty and the pursuit of happiness.' That is perhaps the essence of the conservatism which, in the views of our

108

political philosophers, right, left, and centre, distinguishes the Canadian from the American political tradition. I should perhaps qualify this by speaking of the English-Canadian tradition, but it seems to me that it is the tradition in practice of French Canadians, whose political life has been almost entirely in the British parliamentary model. Although our kind of functionalism often seems to be at war with the more Cartesian language of Quebec intellectuals, Pierre Trudeau used the word 'fonctionelle' to describe the policy he advocates for Quebeckers of accomplishing their aims by doing things rather than by indulging in nationalist rhetoric.[2] It is the tradition of René Lévesque if not the ideologues of his party. Burke, although he didn't like the Quebec Act, described what was to be the Canadian *modus operandi* when he said that government is a 'practical thing, made for the happiness of mankind, and not to furnish out a spectacle of uniformity to gratify the schemes of visionary politicians.'[3]

It is not easy, of course, to cling to home-grown tenets against the constant influence of the American way. 'The "American way of life,"' as Ramsay Cook puts it, 'grew out of the history of the United States, not out of our history.'[4] There is no question of deliberate subversion. Washington could not concentrate its attention on us long enough for that. The Americans cannot control the export of their culture in the way the Japanese put quotas on their cars. And we are not alone as benefactors and victims. American culture is exported world-wide – not imposed but eagerly imported. Even the self-confident French have been alarmed by the promise (or threat) of satellite television and other technological marvels. Two writers in *Le Monde* recently noted the problem as they saw it: 'There is appearing, in various forms, a world cultural market, dominated in fact by the United States. Tomorrow, if we are not careful, we shall have to go to the data bank of the United States Senate or some other private transatlantic company to find out what happened on 14 July 1789. The Americans are gradually robbing us of our memories.'[5]

The threat to Canada is not different, just closer; we are more likely than the Parisians to think Davey Crockett is one of us. But it is our history that made us what we are. If we slip into amnesia or turn on the wrong channel we lose our way. We can blame our own educators to some extent for succumbing to the fashionable thesis that history is something for a modern people to forget. Because nationalism was regarded after the last war as a bad thing, our students were offered a healthful pablum of North American history. There is everything to be said for revealing the War of 1812 as a cruel and deplorable absurdity but not for failing to distinguish between the radically different, though – I hasten to say – equally virtuous, courses of Canadian and American constitutional development.

We are, I think, passing out of that heresy, but damage has been done. Canada as a valid entity is in danger of extinguishing itself in something called North America. Canadian journalists, professors, drama critics talk constantly of our North American cities, North American literature, of continental crime rates, sociological statistics all computed together. I have even had a student speak of our North American system of government. He was astonished to learn that our Canadian system had more in common with those of Germany and Australia than with the United States. There are obviously many quite appropriate ways of talking about North American phenomena, much that is common and coincidental in our patterns of thought and behaviour. But too many Canadians who talk about North America in this way are describing United States phenomena and adding us on without noting our nonconformity.

The recommended alternative is not to claim for Canada just what is virtuous but to recognize and cherish our own variant. The last thing I would advocate is that claustrophobic search for pure Canadian culture, unadulterated by William Shakespeare, which leads only to pre-Inuit artifacts and snow blindness. However, the failure to distinguish Canadian cultural and social qualities when they exist leads not just to a failure of pride but also to false diagnosis and treatment. I recall, for example, arguments with American liberals who regarded it as very reactionary of the Canadian government not to have integrated schools in Quebec.

We must be careful, of course, not to fall into the common error of confusing modernization with Americanization, particularly now when the United States is no longer the clear leader in technology. The Canadian nation is constantly threatened by a ruthless drive towards the most efficient organization of this continent, but the juggernaut is Canadian as well as American in its mindless propulsion. It is a force that is just as characteristic of modern Europe, East and West, and even more dreadfully of the new Asia. When George Grant in the sixties

111

lamented the passing of our nation, crushed by technology, he had a point, but he encouraged an unfortunate tendency to identify the problem with the imperial power of the USA. (Nostalgia is seductive. The Grantian vision of our bucolic Canadian paradise lost is somewhat reminiscent of the lament of the Reaganites for the world of Booth Tarkington and the Land of Oz.)

It is true that super technology and super industrial power as pioneered in America have posed severe challenges to our economic self-government, but in the struggle to civilize these monsters, we and the Americans have a good deal in common. T.P. Loblaw had as much to do with inventing the supermarket as did Messrs A & P. The multinational corporation is less and less an American phenomenon or a tool of Washington. It is an international force in its own right, offering advantage as well as disadvantage, and by no means monolithic in its thrust. Increasingly we, and the Americans as well, have been turning to various UN bodies and the OECD to seek international regulation of these powerful economic forces.

Our more strident anti-Americans of recent vintage overstated the case against American 'domination' to such an extent that they encouraged histrionic despair rather than that pragmatic instinct to cope which has been our salvation. That instinct has, in fact, reversed many of the trends of a decade ago, although Canadians are perversely loath to face up to any good news. Not only has the percentage of foreign control of, for example, our oil industry been declining; our own swashbuckling entrepreneurs seem to be buying up Denver, Dallas, and even Manhattan as well as rebuilding Los Angeles. They even

112

made a pass at such great American institutions as Wool-worth's, provoking, it might be noted, noisy nationalist resistance in the US to foreign ownership, a reaction which we had been told was peculiarly Canadian. North-rop Frye saw in the sobering of the American empire after Vietnam and Watergate indications 'that the American way of life is slowly becoming Canadianized.'[6]

Personally, I found the changed atmosphere of the later seventies, in spite of the well-cultivated gloom, much better than that of the shrill decade. The chastened Americans were considerably more likeable; Canadians probably seemed a little more lovable to them since we revised our expectations and turned some attention to our own sins. We had been breeding a peculiarly obnoxious type of Canadian nationalist who saw our world mission as immaculate sin-resistance. Unlike what has so often been said of the Mexicans, they fancied themselves to be so near to God and so far from the United States. The ultra-nationalist campaign discredited Canadian national-ism by basing it on an unconvincing caricature of Uncle Sam, a handicap now when a healthy stress on our distinct qualities is needed, and a shift in American directions may call for firm but rational resistance.

We suffer somewhat from a failure of the historic sense, a static view of phenomena. We ignore trends or cycles. Consider, for example, our unwitting talk about the Americanization of Canada. Let me cite an English observer in Canada: 'They hope to stop the process which is at present going on of intellectual annexation to the United States.' That was Goldwin Smith writing to Max Müller in 1874.[7] So what is new? Well, one hundred years later another English observer, Clive Barnes, wrote in *The Times* that to a large extent surface similarities are illusory. 'Canada,' he said, 'really is a different nation and seems to be getting more different rather than less. And one of the areas of greatest difference is in the arts.'[8]

It is in any case nonsense to talk about Canada being Americanized when it always has been just as much an American nation as the United States. Our polity is very different. Both peoples brought with them from Europe their experience of government, and there is no reason to claim that the United States way is any more natively North American than the Canadian. The British forms of government which we developed for our own circumstances are not, as sometimes implied, foreign importations. They are as native to us as the ways of Westminster are to present generations of Britons. Governmental institutions spring from a people's heritage, not out of their soil.

The confusion is not all our own fault. In trying to identify ourselves satisfactorily we have had semantic problems we can blame on the inability of our two largest associates to find decent names for themselves. They have had to use as adjectives for themselves, British and American, terms to which we have had also some claim, depending on the context. If the United States had called itself Columbia, leaving the term American for others to share, we could be as comfortable as the Bruxellois are in being Belgians and Europeans.

To get some idea of directions in which we might be moving or cycling, I have been looking again at the considerable amount of self-examination by political theorists that accompanied the centenary of 1967, Expo, and the new régime in Ottawa. Some of it is best forgotten. Along with the healthy birthday glow was a streak of chauvinism that betrayed much insecurity. One reads now with blushes the excited debates in parliament when the *Manhattan* made its way into the Arctic seas in 1969. As editors and MPs saw it, it was rather like the Armada of Spain entering the English Channel. When asked to define 'chauvinism' that great student of language, Denis Norden, responded aptly: 'There's no vinism like chau-vinism.' Just so! The fustian in parliament at that time was rather like Victorian melodrama, with hisses for the villainous Uncle and his wicked agent, Exxon. I like to think that we have grown out of that kind of children's crusade. However, recent tendencies to confuse Margaret Thatcher with the Hanoverians have not been reassuring.

Along with these rushes of blood to the head (which affect all nice nations from time to time) there was also some excellent and judicious analysis of what kind of country we are. I shall cite the words of a selected few who have said what I mean better than I could have done. Of course, I have chosen those I agree with, but they are not isolated or partisan voices.

First, the late W.S. Morton: 'Canadian history is not a parody of American, as Canada is not a second-rate United States, still less a United States that failed. Canadian history is rather an important chapter in a distinct and even an unique human endeavour, the civilization of the northern and arctic lands.'[9] With considerable insight Professor Morton has defined the particular qualities of our heritage from the seacoast settlements of the Northern seas. There has been a mystic quality to our northernness that has inspired and liberated the Canadian soul even though it descends at times into a self-conscious shamanism. However, this mettlesome element is now seriously threatened, I fear, by the Florida sickness which undermines our esprit de corps as well as our economy.

Ramsay Cook, arguing the case for a nation-state without nationalism, recognizes the valid question as to what else could hold together a people as disparate as Canadians. The answer, he says, should be self-evident, 'except for those with an unquenchable thirst for ideological certainty and national purity.' 'The nation-state serves the practical purpose of organizing groups of people into manageable units and providing them with services which they need and which they can share: a railway, a medicare program, a publicly owned broadcasting system, an art gallery, an experimental farm, a manpower retraining program, a guarantee of equality for linguistic rights. Not perhaps the heady stuff from which Garibaldis or Guevaras are made. But, then, Canada is neither a nineteenth-century Italy nor a twentieth-century Cuba.'[10] We are not a nation state in the European tradition. We are a modern state designed to protect and further the interests of diverse peoples not to weld them into some mystical unity. It is a model far more appropriate to the needs of other new states than those which have generated wars over language and totems. For those nationalists who worry about differentiating Canada from the United States, Cook has a formula: 'Canada will *not* be precisely what the United States epitomizes – a nationalist society.'[11]

Some find these counsels tame, but Donald Smiley, with his smooth tongue in his amiable cheek, sees our justification in the old hymn: 'For not with swords loud clashing / Nor roll of stirring drums / But deeds of love and mercy / The heavenly Kingdom comes.'[12] That's us! Like Cook, Smiley feels there is only one Canadian question and that is how those who live within our national boundaries 'can establish and sustain governmental institutions which can be at once humane, effective and responsive.'[13] Such national values and commitments as Canadians have are concretely embodied in particular measures for honouring the mutual claims of citizens and governments or each other. 'If,' he concludes, 'the present claims can be sustained and new claims from time to time added, Canadian nationalism may need nothing more.'[14]

Is this not enough? Our identity for good or ill is assured by our unique heredity and our unique environment. Why still the unquiet spirit, the restless search for a national unity and an immaculate independence that are as unobtainable as they are undesirable? We strain too much. Arthur Lower says Canada is a supreme act of faith.[15] Are we not on firmer ground if we regard it as a hell of a good arrangement – for those lucky enough to be enclosed in it? Because we are unique we have our own values. We should not assess our quality by the standards foreign governments set for themselves. The differences between Canada and the United States are considerably greater than the differences between Cana-

117

dians and Americans, but I shall refrain from setting them out at greater length lest I encourage a kind of introspection the endless perpetuation of which weakens our fibre and bores our friends.

We are a part of North America, but also of the West and of mankind. It would help, to begin with, if we thought of ourselves more often as a unique country in the world at large. If we allow ourselves, as Frank Underhill said, 'to be obsessed by the danger of American cultural annexation, so that the thought preys on us day and night, we shall only become a slightly bigger Ulster.'[16] The whole world has, in fact, been obsessed by the United States whether in admiration, contempt, envy, or horrid fascination. If the Americans have an exaggerated view of their place in the universe, this greatness has to a large extent been thrust upon them. It is no criticism of the United States to say that its excessive role has distorted world order. They themselves, if they can make the necessary psychic adjustment, would be the greatest beneficiaries of their reduction in rank to something more like that of an ordinary country. Canadians, among others, make them extraordinary by our inability to see past them. Our self-destructive obsession with the United States is notable, for example, in our habit of calculating our exchange rates in terms only of the US dollar. The fact that our currency has risen prodigiously in value against the mark, the franc, the yen, and the pound was obscured while we enjoyed in the summer of 1981 an orgy of despair about our economic future in the world.

A constant problem for us is that the United States has always been better theatre. The screen is larger, the sound octophonic, and the media saturation enormous. Hostages can be turned into heroes, and the whole world watches breathlessly. I am not saying that Americans are the world's best dramatists; they just make their life more histrionic. So Canadians with a hunger for drama are seduced, and our sober values deplored. I find 'peace, order and good government' an entirely satisfying goal, and the words to me have a spare elegance that I like to think of as typically Canadian. One of our Canadian film directors, Tom Hedley, thinks otherwise: 'I genuinely believe the United Empire Loyalists came here because they did not believe in pursuing happiness. The Declaration of Independence is about the pursuit of ideas that turn into dreams and neuroses; the BNA Act reads like a real estate document. Americans are able to recycle certain myths over and over again and still hold on to the American dream; Canadians think of defining and redefining myths as a corny and uninteresting exercise. The country's imaginary life is obscured.'[17]

Well, to begin with, our history is largely imaginary. We are great mythmakers but our myths are mostly self-denigrating. One of the myths we cling to, for example, is that Canada is a country of stern puritan tradition, an assumption based on a few phenomena of this century which were in fact reactions against our rip-roaring past. The clean and decent life of Toronto is of late much admired – and exaggerated – by Americans, but there is an increasing tendency on the part of arty Canadians to deplore it. If only we had the violence that lurks in the sleazy decadence of New York, we would have so much better film scripts! There is even a brand of social mor-

119

alists, loudly beating their tin drums, who see in our admired behaviour an oppressively moral society in which dissent is not permitted, discrimination of various kinds is rampant, and everything is swept under the carpet, a society in which we all crouch in fear of the police and the War Measures Act.

These critics have points worth making, and they should never be silenced. There are higher virtues than cleanliness and order; dissenters and minorities need constant protection; and the price of liberty remains eternal vigilance. What is needed, however, is a sense of proportion. Wise and humane government, as tranquil as possible, has been the main aim of civilization for centuries. When the American Association for the Advancement of Science met in Toronto in January, an official took an advance look and reported of this city, 'I have seen civilization, and it works.' Like most of us, I suppose, I found that statement gratifying and embarrassing, knowing how far short of the ideal we fall. Nevertheless, it is a tribute to be pondered. Quiet streets and a city that works may be unfashionable, but they are much valued by those who haven't got them. There are other measures of civilization than the liberality of the liquor laws and the consumption of food and drink on the *trottoirs*. Our civil liberties need reinforcement, but before getting carried away it would be advisable to consult the files of Amnesty International to find out what war measures in peacetime are really like in most parts of the world. Crying 'wolf' has always been a dangerous game.

Would we get better Canadian literature if we identified a Canadian dream and recycled it? Tchekov wrote about human beings in the Russian environment and his plays are never off the world stage – even in the Soviet Union. The first great American novel was about a whale. What we need are more writers who look at the life around them and see it without the distortion of imported glasses – and not always on the steppes of Saskatchewan in the depression. Our film-makers who try to pretend that Toronto is Cincinnati ought to be exiled to Cincinnati. The Australians produce films about their own life and history which are justly admired in Cannes, New York, and Toronto. It is a healthy sign that we now have fewer novelists seeking their Canadian souls in the great epic saga. They are looking around them. More affection is being lavished on our bears and pigs – preferable surely to our really rather nasty beavers. There are, thank God, almost no typical Canadians. Critics have tended to reject Maria Chapdelaine and the Whiteoaks of Jalna as not being typical because they don't fancy them as acceptable stereotypes but surely they are just as typical of our variegated patterns in time and space as Charlie Farquharson, Duddy Kravitz, or the family Plouffe.

I return to the importance of history, of understanding better how we came to be what we are. In doing so I recognize the validity of Harold Innis's argument that 'We must somehow escape on the one hand from an obsession with the moment and on the other hand from our obsession with history.'[18] Perhaps we should just escape from obsession. Is it the pursuit of impossible dreams that has made us mythmakers, concocting whatever history suits our favoured theses – something I recognize that I could be accused of myself? Mr Tom Hedley, I am sure, has never actually studied the Loyalists, many of whom were running away from the puritanism and the dogmatism of revolutionary America. That fascinating and diverse band of refugees has been reconstructed incessantly as villains or heroes and their presumed tradition has been invoked to fit various preposterous arguments. David Bell, in a perceptive examination of the Loyalist tradition, cites Ernest Renan: 'To forget and – I will venture to say – to get one's history wrong, are essential factors in the making of a nation.'[19]

The last thing we want is an authorized version of Canada's history. In any case no one is likely to reconcile Professor Creighton with Professor Lower or either with Professor Brunet. Some agreed interpretations are required for survival. It is all to the good that we do steadily, in English and to some extent in French Canada, maintain the tradition of honouring and linking Wolfe and Montcalm, Baldwin and Lafontaine, Macdonald and Cartier – as statues or highways. It is a legitimate interpretation of our history for somewhat didactic purposes, a matter of arranging rather than distorting the facts.

On the whole historians have a hard time persuading us that we are a success. We feel defenceless without our grievances, seeing ourselves as children battered by Mother and Uncle and probably illegitimate. The American tradition, as we know, was to believe they never lost a war. We cling to the belief that we have never gained a victory. Queenston Heights, I admit, may be nothing to boast about, but we might look back more smugly at the many times we peacefully defied the Americans without losing our inheritance. We established ourselves in the nineteenth century on the 49th instead of the 54th parallel. Somewhat more to the present point we out-manoeuvred them over the St Lawrence Seaway in the fifties and Paul Martin defied them over the admission of new members to the UN. In the seventies we stared them down over their surcharge on imports and calmly risked their vehement protests by our Arctic Waters Pollution Prevention Act. I could go on.

Everybody has a theory about the cause of our acne. I suggest that it is partly because we are at war with our past. We judge it harshly out of fierce convictions about the present instead of caressing it all fondly as part of our growing up. It all happened, for good or ill, and this rich land is the product. All our yesterdays are part of us. Why have we been prevented by prejudice and counter-prejudice from looking, for example, at that Loyalist trek as an extraordinary human experience – *Doctor Zhivago* and *Gone with the Wind*? In the fascinating capitals of Europe with their gorgeous histories and tourist brochures we find squares and statues honouring whoever passed by: liberators, tyrants, poets of one bloody reign or another. (Every time a statue is proposed in Toronto there is a row, whether it is Edward VII or Sun Yat Sen.) The British weave their rich history out of Celts and Saxons, Danes and Normans, and cherish their Roman ruins. The Americans even fly the old British flag over Williamsburg and the fleur de lis over Fort Niagara. In spite of brave and frightfully self-conscious efforts to salvage us some heroes along the way, we seem to think our history is something to be ashamed of.

We now glorify our multiculture, adding thereby a liberating perspective to our national life. There is a tendency, however, to over-compensate by rejecting as unnative the British traditions that came with us and gave us shape. Take, for example, the renunciation of Dominion Day. What began as a celebration of national exuberance, of the extension of our dominion from sea to sea in almost blasphemous terms and in defiance of the US secretary of state, is completely misinterpreted as a badge of colonial shame. There was certainly a time, some years ago, when the word dominion had become anachronistic for our altered condition and we dropped it. But can we not celebrate great events along the way? Canada, as a dominion, provided the term and status which led other colonies to self-government. And why not Victoria Day as well? That lady played a great part in the life of nineteenth-century Canadians – not consciously, of course; she never came near the country. It was not the empress of India or the widow of Windsor but the queen of Canada, an invention of our own, a really fun queen who gave us holidays and fireworks and nice statues in the parks. Ontario in particular was shaped in the Victorian mould; it is part of our fabric. That is no argument, of course, against the québécois preference for celebrating St Jean Baptiste instead. He never visited us either, but he is part of our fabric.

Since at least 1603 Canadians have been weaving a tapestry to be enjoyed in tranquillity. In recent years we have been expanding our vision to grasp the riches of the earlier heritage of our native peoples. To see all this as a long struggle for liberation from something or other is to deny our heritage. Jules Léger, who was always at ease with being Canadian, pointed out in his first speech as governor general that we had been formed and sometimes deformed by English, French, and American influences. 'But now,' he added, 'we have the strength, the numbers and the self-confidence to choose what suits us, to assimilate it and give it originality, thus creating a civilization of many cultures.' Why not a statue for him with those words engraved on it?

Are we ashamed of our past because the contagious American tradition and the twentieth-century Zeitgeist have persuaded us to see ourselves in the guise of anti-colonialists? Then indeed, as the Frenchmen said, the Americans are robbing us of our memories. Struggling for liberation from an imperial yoke may seem more exciting than the slow working out by mutual agreement of the forms of self-government, but it is not the history of Canada. I know that the old history with all that talk about the winning of responsible government got boring and self-righteous, but good government, the greatest need of mankind in 1981, is the boring kind of government. The formula we and the British invented was applied worldwide to the largest of the empires and saved the world from many Vietnams. How very boring! Ours has been, in fact, the colonial struggle in reverse. It was we who clung to the British connection to serve our own needs as a counterweight to a powerful neighbour or a court of appeal from our own indecision. We are still embarrassing the British government long after they had liberated themselves from all their troublesome colonies except Canada and Belize.

Even though it has been repeated ad nauseam, one must still make the case that the achievement of self-government by evolution and peaceful negotiation is a better lesson for the present century than achieving it by mob and musket. One need not make it an anti-American argument, however. The Thirteen Colonies would undoubtedly have preferred that route themselves. We were fortunate enough to deal with the British after they had learned the lesson of 1776. We owe the Americans a good deal for showing us the way how to do things – and also how not to do them. One could cite a civil war, prohibition, and urban expressways – not to mention 'the division of powers.'

In our relations with the United States, furthermore, doctrinaire theories of imperialism and dependence are too often misapplied. What about Canadian imperialism in contest with American? There were certainly elements of that in our push to the west and more than a hint of 'manifest destiny' in the National Policy. We are no more virtuous, just different. Seeing our history through American prisms is as dangerous to our self-awareness as tacking habits of the US presidential system, however effective in their own context, on to a parliamentary system which they could seriously distort. There is much more than sentiment involved in getting our history straight; it is a question of survival. A nation, even a bi-national nation, is a living organism.

The Continuing Relationship

The late Marcel Cadieux, who was one of our toughest and wisest ambassadors to the US, said once when asked what could be done to improve the relationship: 'It's quite simple. All you have to do is change the American constitution.' It is, and always has been, an uphill struggle all the way, but in conclusion I should like to pull myself together and express confidence in both Canadians and Americans to find ways and means of living for many more years out of wedlock and of adjusting to our changing estates in the family of nations. We have been distinct communities on this continent since the early seventeenth century, and at the age of nearly 400 each it is a time for maturity rather than senility. The Americans have aged rapidly in the past decade and might be expected to regard us more maturely if we could catch their eye. As for us, we have matured somewhat from the unreal arguments of the sixties about independence and domination to a more precise vocabulary and analysis, but there are still signs of adolescence.

With due provocation the irascible British critic, Bernard Levin, once said at an Ottawa conference on the arts, 'The next person who refers to Canada as "a young country" I shall hit – providing he is smaller than I am.'[1] It has been a fallacious excuse for mediocrity. Our political life is at least as old as Magna Carta and we can count Chaucer and Rabelais among our cultural forefathers, however un-Canadian they might seem to the likes of Mr Hedley. With multiculturalism now declared as official doctrine, we perhaps have a lien also on a whole range of stars, from Dante Alighieri to Lao-Tse. Why not?

With our penchant for despair we lose sight of our Canadian genius for creating new forms to accommodate differing peoples, our own faltering but path-making experiment in confederation, our decisive role in creating a Commonwealth of Nations. Our present floundering should be judged in the light of the boldness of our design, the incomparable endeavour to tame a vast space and to create a new kind of modern international state. We fail to give ourselves credit perhaps because our concepts did not proceed from the elegant rhetoric of anthologized philosophers like Burke or Jefferson. They evolved from a perspicacious sense for the required adaptation of ends to means, a native instinct for 'peace, order and good government.' Our way was to start from the historic predicament rather than the teachings of Plato, making things work, going for the pragmatic solution but with an eye on the longer-range consequences, and then finding an appropriately moral philosophy to help the citizenry like and appreciate what they had to live with. 'The American,' according to H.L. Mencken, 'seeks to escape from the soluble by pretending that it is solved.'[2] Our very sensible process has, of course, been exceedingly raucous at times like the present. The derived philosophy of functionalism Canadian-style has perhaps been a little smug. It was intended to give Canadians more confidence in their own workmanlike way of doing things. The danger is that it encourages complacency and discourages boldness. We can do with a cautious rashness. Adversity has sobered Canadians from the extravagant controversies of nationalists and anti-nationalists of a few years ago. There were real issues at stake, but it often seemed like a conflict of metaphors. One vague notion, continentalism, became a meaningless term of abuse. It is a word that could be endowed with useful meaning some time but might better be excluded from present debate. We could do also without the Marxist and anti-Marxist dialectics which, valuable though they may be in certain circumstances, have too often distorted a special relationship they did not fit. Which is not to say that there cannot be a Marxist interpretation of the relationship between Canadian and American imperialisms that is worth listening to – provided it recognizes the difference between Canada and Nicaragua.

The present search has been enormously helped by a new brand of Canadian scholars, and even some American professors who now recognize that the relationship is at least intellectually interesting. Systemic definitions, more exact contemplation of phenomena, and more value-free research will lead us, one can hope, to better ways of understanding and of managing an international association that is *sui generis* but not without interest to the world at large. We have been through worse periods in our past two-and-a-half centuries of living with the South. We have not lost our inventive touch. In September 1980, for example, not only Canada and the US but also Saskatchewan and Montana came up with a shrewd proposal for a monitoring arrangement in the joint tradition on the Poplar River Power Plant which had provoked a good deal of shouting across the 49th parallel. It may seem a small thing but our transborder agenda is a multitude of such small things. Our search is not for solutions but for ungrandiose schemes.

The historian, Gerald Craig, said of our predicament after Confederation: 'The fundamental requirement for Canadian-American friendship would be recognition of the inequality of power between the two federations.'[3] It seems obvious enough, but we forget too easily what it means. So far we have cannily seen the difference between those concepts which promise shared rule over the continent and those which are sturdily joint. We would be wise to keep that difference clearly in mind now when the times are, so to speak, out of joint. Should we perhaps favour the kind of institutions that the Scandinavians maintain for maximum co-operation without loss of sovereignty? These are instruments that can be used selectively. They are available but they don't have to be used. The word most frequently employed now in describing the North American requirement is 'management.' The essence of those mislaid fisheries agreements was joint management of fish stocks which we have a common interest in maintaining. That is another reason for Ottawa's lament over their rejection. Managing fish, however, is one thing. Setting up some grand body to manage North America is another. Without any voting power what leverage would we have?

Much nonsense is talked about the end of a special relationship between Canada and the United States. It is and always will be a special relationship requiring unique definitions, but it can change. All bilateral relationships between countries are special. There is certainly a special relationship between the United States and the Soviet Union, recognized particularly in their bilateral negotiations on strategic arms limitation and in their attention to signals between them. I would not press the comparison with the Canada-US relationship except for the element of paradox in both. The US and the USSR are in competition, constantly struggling for advantage, but recognizing certain limits, recognizing, in fact, a common cause in the prevention of nuclear war. Our Canada-US common causes are much broader and deeper, but there is and must remain the freedom to compete and struggle for advantage as well as co-operate.

My inclination, as I have been saying, is to believe that our endeavours should be towards clearer understandings along with, if they are useful, institutions that facilitate co-operation but stake out fences. Amalgation is more likely to come about incrementally than intentionally. Definition helps us to know where we stand. As Carl Berger has said, 'to understand limits is to enhance the freedom of the nation and the individual.'[4]

We dare not ignore the revolutionary implications of the cybernetic age, but we ought not to be hypnotized by it. Integration is not a force to which we meekly or enthusiastically surrender our will. It requires discipline, lest we all get mashed. Nor should we jump too quickly to conclusions as to where we are heading. It is not all in one direction. Consider, for example, the following comment by John Crispo on one important area where integration of some kind has been in existence for about a century. 'The trend towards Canadianization within international unions should set the stage for an appropriate combination of international solidarity and national autonomy. If that is the ultimate effect in North America, truly international unions crossing many borders may become viable.'[5] As Joseph Nye of Harvard has commented: 'The advanced industrial world may be a world of transnational relations, but so far the transnational world of North America is not a postnationalist world. The eagle may soar; beavers build dams.'[6]

We might consider more carefully the posture we adopt when we make requests or demands of the US, the tone of our arguments. We have a historic habit of seeing our positions as grievances or complaints. Sometimes we have indeed been wronged, but most of the time we are dealing with a clash of legitimate interests. The peevish tone leaves the impression we seek indulgences. What we want is an equitable relationship, intricate and complex, of two disparate states. Even when we seek the necessary protections for a more vulnerable culture and economy we ask for a functional approach to specific predicaments, not kindly concessions to the weak. Strength and weakness are facts of life, not evidence of injustice. We do not ask the Americans to stop bullying us but to consider conflicts of interest on their merits. Fortunately there are some areas in which the Americans need that kind of consideration from us. The matter may seem unimportant, but

132

Americans on the whole, and with justification, do not feel that they mistreat Canada. They react defensively – and sometimes offensively – to the implication that they have done us wrong. It is, of course, not easy to get them to see how they can wrong us inadvertently. Injured innocence is not the best tack to get them to the table. It is demeaning for a country of our advanced age and vast resources to regard itself as a weak sister, pushed around. We don't look hungry enough to be convincing. If the Americans are to regard us more maturely, then we must cast off the image of dependence.

I have tried also to suggest that in calculating our own relationship with the United States we must bear in mind the responsibilities of that country in the world at large. To understand their role in proper perspective I have linked it to our vision of world order after the war. In defining the place of the United States we could not avoid contradiction then as now. The difference in power, both military and economic, was enormous, a basic fact of life none of us had willed and to which we all had to accommodate ourselves. A more nicely balanced world would have been neater to make schemes for, but in desperate times there was even something to be said for a boss state. The way the United States used its power did matter, but there was nothing they could do to make themselves more equal – even if they again opted out of the world body. The problems of great and lesser powers co-operating or arguing, are inherent. Striking the David vs Goliath posture or berating the great powers in general is a form of scapegoating. The smaller power cannot avoid involvement in the consequence of the great power's actions and it wants, therefore, to share in the decisions that lead to the consequences. But most formulas for sharing are a delusion because it is the power with the resources that has to accept the responsibility for decision. We must live with that quandary.

To illustrate I might cite a notable case. Canadians complained, and with justification, that, in accordance with the terms of the NORAD agreement, we should have been consulted before the Kennedy government took its bold decision to cope with the Soviet missiles in Cuba in 1962. Yet one must ask what we could possible have said or done if we had been represented in those intense and heated and ultra-secret discussions in Washington while the Americans decided what to do about their forces and only marginally ours. As Mackenzie King had earlier realized, it was perhaps better not to be consulted because then one was not automatically committed to agree and to participate. There are always ways and means of making one's views known – if not in moments of crisis, at least when positions are being prepared – and the ways and means are best not prescribed. The inequality must be accepted, philosophically but not meekly. Not even the superpowers, after all, can get their own way. It is well to bear in mind that, whatever the NORAD agreement might seem to have implied, we had maintained diplomatic and commercial relations with Cuba contrary to the wishes of Washington. We recognized that our security was linked but we both retained the right to determine when and how our security was threatened.

We have needed the United States for the world order we considered essential for our own interests. In the early years it acted as a kind of surrogate United Nations, paying for those things others could or would not pay for, providing the logistic base or the deterrent force essential for the rudimentary efforts to keep the peace. It often took decisions without due consultation, but sometimes it did so because action had been stalemated by collective indecision. While furthering a world order favourable to their own interests, the Americans believed that all countries would profit from the spill-over and the trickle-down. So did we.

There are grounds for complaint here, but Canada has less grounds than most. The world vision was short-sighted in many respects. There were unforeseen consequences, and the benefits were grossly uneven, but it was certainly not only the United States or the Western countries which profited from the enormous impetus to production and exchange that followed the war or the relative peace provided by the American deterrent. In hindsight it is wise to stare hard at the alternatives actually possible at the time. We were all, furthermore, in a very unsophisticated stage in comprehending how to build a better economic order and keep the peace.

The American dream for the world was one in which we half believed. The moral arrogance was hard to take, but Canadians had learned over many years to greet Fourth of July oratory with appropriate scepticism and appropriate respect. The Americans would have to be reminded firmly and constantly that they had no monopoly on righteousness or wisdom. They were more deficient in the latter than in the former. Still, theirs was a much more acceptable kind of imperialism than what the Nazis or

Stalinists offered. In stark terms we would support them not because we were on their side but because we wanted them on our side. It was particularly essential that they prop up the new world order, the UN and NATO and the rest of the structure, until we could get it running on more equitable and enduring principles. I have little doubt in retrospect that we were right under the circumstances in accepting American leadership thus, with reservations, and that history will, with some severe reprimands, consider that the United States justified our faith by its part in establishing a new order. It is a fact to conjure with, however, that our confidence in the American dream has been seriously qualified in recent years by its realizing itself in unexpected and unpleasant ways not only abroad but at home in those glittering cities we used to emulate. 'How strange and unfamiliar it is,' wrote Dalton Camp in the autumn of 1980, 'to look upon the Great Republic without awe, admiration, or envy, but with unease, dismay, and perhaps pity.'[7]

The United States of America is greater than any administration, and its progress has always been cyclical. Many administrations have scared us, but we have found new terms of agreement. Dr Jekyll usually triumphs. The schizophrenia of America is well described by Raymond Aron. Looking back to the divided support for the war with Mexico, he noted 'certain traits characteristic of the external action of the United States to this day, such as the flare-up of public opinion ... legalistic scruples, the swing between the will to power (or expansion) and an uneasy conscience, and a curious mixture of pragmatic and moralistic morality.'[8] Come to think of it, there may be something to be said for digging up our wars. Testimony to the moral quality of the Americans is the very poor show they made of their two invasions of Canada. Their hearts weren't really in them. They have an imperial flare, but they are not, thank God, very good imperialists in the long run.

The American sin was not selfishness but hubris. I wonder if we might have done more to restrain their excesses, to help them learn how to live with the poor and work with their peers. We have our own sour reputation for nauseous holiness and hypocrisy to cope with, our rhetoric too often outpacing our contribution. Dean Acheson, whose parents were part of the Toronto Establishment, resented the homilies Canadian ambassadors were constantly delivering to him, urging him to do things he was trying his damdest to do. He later wrote an essay about Canada called 'Stern Daughter of the Voice of God.' Could we, nevertheless, as best friends, have prepared them better for the resentments that now overwhelm and discourage them by pointing out how we have resented and respected them for two centuries?

Americans, of course, would furiously resent this kind of condescending talk from a small and backward neighbour, but they talk that way all the time about other mixed-up peoples they sincerely want to help. They need best friends to tell them when their breath is bad. The fanatical anti-Americanism which has become such a destructive force in the world threatens not just the United States but world equilibrium. We remain Number One exhibit to prove that American influence is limited by moral inhibitions. To make that point convincingly, how-

137

ever, we have to continue being not a submissive but a stubborn, opinionated, tiresome, and, of course, always wise friend. We have to protect our heritage to show the world that on the borders of at least one superpower, that can be done. It can't be done, however, unless the Americans climb off their godlike perch to see Canada as it really is and see it steadily and see it whole.

Notes

INTRODUCTION

1 *New York Times*, 1 Feb. 1931

CHAPTER 1: ALSO PRESENT AT THE CREATION

1 A.E. Gotlieb, 'Benjamin Franklin and the East Coast
  Fisheries Agreement,' Algonquin College, International
  Seminar, Ottawa, 21 Oct. 1980
2 J.W. Pickersgill, *The Mackenzie King Record*. I: *1930-
  1944* (Toronto 1960), 430
3 Denis Brogan, 'An Outsider Looking In,' Canada's
  Tomorrow Conference, Quebec, 13-14 Nov. 1953
4 '*Article 2*
  The Parties will contribute toward the further development of peaceful and friendly international relations by
  strengthening their free institutions, by bringing about a
  better understanding of the principles upon which these
  institutions are founded, and by promoting conditions of
  stability and well-being. They will seek to eliminate
  conflict in their international economic policies and will
  encourage economic collaboration between any or all of
  them.' *NATO Facts and Figures* (Brussels 1976), 300

CHAPTER 2: SHAPING THE CONTINENT

1 Sperry Lea, confidential memorandum to the author

2 'The following principles are established for the purpose of facilitating these objectives:

1. In order to achieve an optimum production of goods essential for the common defence, the two countries shall develop a co-ordinated programme of requirements, production and procurement.

2. To this end, the two countries shall, as it becomes necessary, institute co-ordinated controls over the distribution of scarce raw materials and supplies.

3. Such United States and Canadian emergency controls shall be mutually consistent in their objectives, and shall be so designed and administered as to achieve comparable effects in each country. To the extent possible, there shall be consultation to this end prior to the institution of any system of controls in either country which affects the other.

4. In order to facilitate essential production, the technical knowledge and productive skills involved in such production within both countries shall, where feasible, be freely exchanged.

5. Barriers which impede the flow between Canada and the United States of goods essential for the common defence effort should be removed as far as possible.

6. The two governments, through their appropriate agencies, will consult concerning any financial or foreign exchange problems which may arise as a result of the implementation of this agreement.'

'Canada-United States Economic Co-operation,' *External Affairs*, II, Nov. 1950, 414-15

3 See, for example, Joseph S. Nye, Jr, 'Transnational Relations and Interstate Conflicts: An Empirical Analysis,' in Annette Baker Fox, et al, eds., *Canada and the United States: Transnational and Transgovernmental Relations* (New York 1976), 365-402.

1 'Approaches to Foreign Policy: Differences and Similarities,' Department of External Affairs, *Statements and Speeches*, 80/22, 3

2 Lloyd N. Cutler, 'To Form a Government,' *Foreign Affairs*, LIX, fall 1980, 126-7

3 Ibid., 135

4 William Diebold, Jr, 'Canadian-American Relations in a Changing World Economy,' Centre for International Studies, University of Toronto, 1979, 14

5 See Erik B. Wang, 'Canada-United States Fisheries and Maritime Boundary Negotiations: Diplomacy in Deep Water,' *Behind the Headlines*, XXXVIII(6) / XXXIX(1), April 1981.

6 See, for example, Don Munton, 'Dependence and Interdependence in Transboundary Environmental Relations,' *International Journal*, XXXVI, winter 1980-1.

7 A.E. Gotlieb, 'Benjamin Franklin and the East Coast Fisheries Agreement,' Algonquin College, International Seminar, Ottawa, 21 Oct. 1980

8 'U.S. asks France to postpone acquisition of Texasgulf by ELF,' *New York Times*, 21 July 1981

9 John Kirton, 'Canada and the United States: A More Distant Relationship,' *Current History*, LXXIX, Nov. 1980, 117

10 Cited in Ronald Anderson, 'U.S. actions on trade could inhibit Canada,' *Globe and Mail*, 23 July 1980

11 Diebold, 'Canadian-American Relations,' 9, 10

12 'Canada's foreign investment policies called discriminatory to U.S.,' *Globe and Mail*, 21 July 1981, B6

13 Maxwell Cohen, 'Constants and Variables in Canada-United States Relations,' *International Perspectives*, Nov./Dec., 1980, 3-9

14 Canada, Standing Senate Committee on Foreign Affairs,

Minutes of the Fourth Proceedings on Canadian Relations with the United States, 5 June 1980

15 See, for example, Geoffrey Stevens, 'Council of North America,' *Globe and Mail,* 26 Nov. 1980.

16 'Challenges and Opportunities of having the U.S. as a Neighbour,' *Statements and Speeches,* 80/21, 17 Oct. 1980

CHAPTER 4: ON BEING AN ALLY

1 Frank Underhill, *In search of Canadian Liberalism* (Toronto 1960), 262

2 Mark MacGuigan, 'Approaches to Foreign Policy: Differences and Similarities,' Department of External Affairs, *Statements and Speeches,* 80/22, 18 Oct. 1980

CHAPTER 5: CANADA'S ROOTS

1 Northrop Frye, 'Conclusion,' in Carl F. Klinck, ed., *Literary History of Canada: Canadian Literature in English* (Toronto 1976, 2nd ed.), 325-6

2 Cited in Ramsay Cook, *The Maple Leaf Forever* (Toronto 1971), 42

3 Cited in Donald C. Story, 'Government – a "Practical Thing": Towards a Consensus on Foreign Policy Jurisdiction,' in R.B. Byers and Robert W. Reford, eds., *Canada Challenged: The Viability of Confederation* (Toronto 1979), 108

4 Cook, *The Maple Leaf Forever,* 5

5 J.-H. Lorenzi et E. Le Boucher, 'Menace américaine sur la culture,' *Le Monde,* 1 Sept. 1979, ix (my translation)

6 Frye, in *Literary History of Canada,* 327

7 Quoted in Frank Underhill, *In Search of Canadian Liberalism* (Toronto 1960), 93

8 'Canada: searching for an art identity,' *The Times* (London), 24 July 1976

9 William Morton, 'The Northern Frontier: Key to Canadian History,' in William Kilbourn, ed., *Canada: A Guide to the Peaceable Kingdom* (Toronto 1970), 282

10 Cook, *The Maple Leaf Forever*, 8, 9

11 Ibid., 196

12 Donald Smiley, *Canada in Question: Federalism in the 70s* (Toronto 1976, 2nd ed.), 219

13 Ibid., 228

14 Ibid., 219

15 Arthur R.M. Lower, *Colony to Nation: A History of Canada* (Don Mills 1964, 4th rev. ed.), 564

16 Cited by William Kilbourn, 'Two Styles of Historian: Donald Creighton and Frank Underhill,' in *A Guide to the Peaceable Kingdom*, 279

17 In 'A rare man in these graceless times,' *Globe and Mail*, 5 April 1980

18 Carl Berger, *The Writing of Canadian History: Aspects of English-Canadian Historical Writing: 1900 to 1970* (Toronto 1976), 190

19 David Bell, 'The Loyalist Tradition in Canada,' *Journal of Canadian Studies*, v, May 1970, 22

THE CONTINUING RELATIONSHIP

1 'Canada: searching for an art identity,' *The Times* (London), 24 July 1976

2 H.L. Mencken, *The American Scene: A Reader* (New York 1965), 112

3 Gerald Craig, *The United States and Canada* (Cambridge, Mass. 1968), 149

4 Carl Berger, *The Writing of Canadian History: Aspects of English-Canadian Historical Writing, 1900 to 1970* (Toronto 1976), 111

5 *Globe and Mail*, 8 Jan. 1981

6 Joseph S. Nye, Jr, 'Transnational Relations and Interstate Conflicts: An Empirical Analysis,' in Annette Baker

Fox, et al, eds., *Canada and the United States: Transnational and Transgovernmental Relations* (New York 1976), 402

7 Dalton Camp, 'End of the Dream,' *Saturday Night*, XCIV, Nov. 1980, 50

8 Raymond Aron, *The Imperial Republic: The United States and the World, 1945-1973* (Cambridge, Mass. 1974), xxviii